Single Moms Raising Sons

Preparing Boys to Be Men
When There's No Man Around

Dana S. Chisholm

BEACON HILL PRESS
OF KANSAS CITY

Copyright 2007
By Dana S. Chisholm

ISBN-13: 978-0-8341-2308-3
ISBN-10: 0-8341-2308-8

Printed in the
United States of America

Cover Design: J.R. Caines
Interior Design: Sharon Page

10 9 8 7 6 5 4 3 2

Dedication

This book is dedicated to

   . . . my two sons, Christopher and Nathan. You will be wonderful husbands and fathers someday as you model your perfect Father in heaven.

   . . . the boys and men I talked with who graciously shared your stories. You are awesome men of God. Your moms did a great job.

   . . . the mothers and grandmothers who are keeping your eyes on the Lord and know that with Him you can raise good men. Do not grow weary.

Contents

"Forgetting what is behind and straining toward what is ahead, I press on toward the goal to win the prize for which God has called me heavenward in Christ Jesus" (Phil. 3:13-14).

Introduction

Moms can raise great sons. Even when others say the odds are against you, I'm telling you it can be done. I applaud you, and I encourage you to keep going! According to the Census Bureau, 19.8 million children are living with single parents, and 83% of these—or 16.5 million—are living with their mothers.

Encouragement is very popular in society today. We encourage everything from weight loss and exercise to mammograms and colonoscopies. We encourage drinking more water, improving your diet, tolerance, even disaster preparedness. We encourage taking care of the earth, listening to your "inner voice," and public service.

It seems to me, however, that encouragement for moms raising boys on their own is in short supply. Instead, it seems that society's attitude is that boys raised in homes without dads are somehow doomed. By choosing to encourage moms raising boys, whatever their situation—death of the dad, divorce, military service—we are, in fact, strengthening tomorrow's men and fathers.

The Wake-Up Call

The lack of encouragement from society is subtle. It bothered me for a long time before I was able to identify it. It was just little things like the change of tone in one's voice when he or she discovers I'm a single mom. "Ohhhhh, I see."

What do you see? Just a moment ago my boys seemed normal to you, and now that you know I'm a single mom, my boys are carrying baggage they weren't carrying before. It's as if it is a given that morals are lacking in our home, that the boys are really rampaging hellions, and that the person must have caught them on one of their rare good days.

Or the look that goes with, "Oh, your job is the hardest. I don't know how you do it!" The look and the comment are tinged with pity.

I have caught myself trying to keep my situation quiet. As long as people think I'm married and that there is a father in the home, they assume the best of my boys. There is no baggage for them to lug around. I guess I'm hoping that if they get to know us and see that we're normal and have plenty of moral fiber, their misconceptions about the failures of single moms raising sons can be dispelled.

Inevitably, when someone finds out I'm a single mom, the first question is, "Do you have men in their lives who can teach them to be men? You know, good role models for them?"

I wasn't quite putting it all together until one day I was sitting in a lecture hall with 150 other people listening to a talk about why we should be teaching abstinence in our schools. I agreed with what the speaker said. I work with women who are experiencing unplanned pregnancies, and I teach abstinence to teens. The speaker began to quote statistics that supported her statements, and that also sounded reasonable.

I was still with her when she used statistics to prove why marriage is good for our society. I like marriage. I wouldn't mind being married again, and I hope I have raised my sons to be good husbands in good marriages in the future. Marriage is a good thing. As she continued, though, I began to hear what others in the room didn't seem to notice. She started using statistics to prove why every family combination outside of a two-parent family was a failure and would produce kids who were failures. I began to think: *My sons aren't failures. I know many single moms, so statistically I should know many single moms whose boys are failures.*

Then the speaker brushed over a few statistics that jumped out at me. The study she was citing showed that kids from two-parent homes where both parents were involved in their kids' lives did better at staying off drugs, remaining abstinent, not smoking, and steering clear of violence. The group that didn't do well was the group where neither parent was involved in their kids' lives. Both the two-parent homes and the single-parent homes turned out kids who were likely to exhibit the behaviors described above—if the parents were uninvolved.

And I said to myself, *So it's involvement that makes the difference.* Even two-parent homes that lacked parental involvement did badly in this study. That said to me that I have a chance—the slightest hope—of raising boys who won't fail at life. I decided to search out other factors to give me hope for raising great sons.

What defines this involvement that proves to be the key to success? I started interviewing every unmarried mom I could find—and they are everywhere. I met moms who are remarried (now in blended families), moms currently raising boys on their own, and even men who chimed in because they had been raised in what society calls "broken homes."

A Broken Home

Broken home. Now there's a term I hate.

Labels are dangerous. During the '80s, when the bombing of abortions clinics and the shooting of doctors who performed abortions were occurring with some regularity, the local paper in Southern California called me for a quote because of my work with women facing crises such as unplanned pregnancies.

In the story they were planning to run in the paper, the reporter was going to refer to bombers as "pro-life," and asked me if he could quote me as saying I was pro-life. I said "No. you may not say I am pro-life. You may say that I believe abortion hurts women and ends the life of a child." That isn't what the reporter wanted. He wanted someone to say he or she was pro-life because in his story the bombers were also pro-life. But that label, especially for this particular story, carried baggage that was not part of the definition of "pro-life" to me. To the reporter, pro-life meant clinic bomber, doctor killer, and injuring innocent bystanders. I was not going to agree to that label.

My home will not be labeled "broken" if I can help it. Many people consider a broken home to be anything other than a father, a mother, and 2.5 kids. But to me, broken means *dysfunctional*—whether there are two parents in the home or just one. If you ask me if I have a broken home, my answer is that I do not. But you can quote me as saying that, although I'm not married, our home has a Husband and a Father, a Head of the Home. When God is in the picture, the home is always *complete.*

Healthy Home

When I started taking a closer look at the statistics and what was different about my home and all the homes that are successfully raising wonderful sons, I realized there was one common factor: faith. I even found a study or two that showed religion was a positive influence in people's lives. I didn't find a study that compared and contrasted single and married parenting and how religion played a role. But my case studies—interviewing successful single moms—certainly proved to me that the secret to a healthy home is making it complete. That requires a Husband and Father, but I don't mean just finding a man. I mean finding God the Father who promises to be the defender of the widow and father to the fatherless.

Time after time, in homes that seemed to be beating the odds and having success raising boys, the significant factor was they were homes where God was invited in— into the lives of the mothers and into the sons' lives, and God was the role model in those homes.

Honoring the Heroes

Our country is serious about honoring heroes. As a nation, we learned this lesson the hard way during and following our involvement in the Vietnam War. Since that time, we have guarded against treating our military with anything other than the utmost respect. We learned that no matter what we believe about any current war, the men and women serving are to be respected and honored for putting their lives on the line for our freedom. Society is learning a similar lesson regarding moms parenting alone. We are learning that no matter what we think about "broken homes" and the way things *ought* to be, we must honor the individual who is fighting the good fight for her kids each and every day.

When military ships bring our troops home these days, there are great welcoming parties waiting on the docks with banners and bands and families and kisses. If a baby has been born while the father was away, the new dads are the first to get off the ship as thousands look on, eagerly anticipating their own reunions. They are cheered and encouraged as heroes.

We live in San Diego, a huge military town, and we witness these welcoming events regularly. In fact, the reason we live in San Diego is because of the 20 years my father spent in the Navy. We never moved because he was stationed at one of the many bases in the area, so I didn't have to deal with constantly being uprooted and sent to the next duty station. Instead, my dad was almost always deployed somewhere. His longest deployment was an 11-

month stretch. My mom was, for all practical purposes, a single mom raising kids. Each time Dad was deployed, Mom was left at home with three small children—one of which was a boy. That boy, my brother, is now a doctor in the Navy. He turned out to be quite an awesome man—a hero in his own right. I am definitely a proud sister, because he is a wonderful father, husband, and brother. I consider him a hero.

My brother is an emergency room doctor. And although it took me many years to get it through my head, emergency room doctoring is a specialty unto itself. He's not going to grow up and become some other type of doctor. It's emergency medicine, and it's stressful and intense. My brother always says I'm smarter than he is, but he works at it harder. That's why he made it through science and medical school; and he gives me a hard time for my bachelors in communication studies and my masters in organizational leadership. Those aren't "real" sciences, he teases. I have put my training to good use in the nonprofit world, though, by helping women who are experiencing unplanned pregnancies. My brother questions the not-for-profit concept as a whole, but especially helping women choose adoption and parenting instead of abortion.

My family is very close, and we get together most weekends to barbeque and hang out. One weekend my brother joined us and was a little stressed about the rotation he was on at the time. He exclaimed, "It's not like it's easy. People die if I mess up!" I looked at him and simply said, "Me too." He finally got it.

One Hero's Story

I have been leading small groups for women's Bible studies in my home for years. Usually I have single moms in my groups, and I invite them to bring their kids and let them play in another room during Bible study. For a single mother, lack of child care is often an obstacle to attending. In one group, a young mom, 21-year-old Rachel, had joined and showed up faithfully with her two-year-old son, Dylan. The father of the boy was in and out of the picture, but mostly out. He could not be relied upon for financial support—let alone emotional support, nor was he a good role model for Dylan. I shared with the group that I had faced an unplanned pregnancy myself, so Rachel shared her story.

She came from a strong Christian family and had attended the same church her whole life. When she was soon to graduate from high school and head to a private Christian college in September, bad decisions resulted in an unplanned pregnancy. Although the school has since changed its policy, when she told the Christian college she was scheduled to attend about her pregnancy, she was told that this college wasn't the right place for her, derailing her plans.

This young mom is a hero—not only to the two year old toddling around my living room—but to me and all of us. In the face of adversity, she chose the road less traveled, the more difficult one. She chose to do the right thing. Now she is raising a son, working two jobs, and planning to go back to school to become a nurse. That is character. That is being a hero.

Supporting Each Other

Proverbs 27:17 says: "As iron sharpens iron, so one man sharpens another." Our Bible study group helps give us the courage to continue on in our heroic roles. Bible study is one way to gather friends around you who can cheer you on and welcome you home to a safe place when the battle gets tough.

One of my favorite ways to recharge is to go down to the local deli and pick up a white chocolate mocha. My life is crazy busy. Sometimes there's hardly room on my calendar to tend to the basics of life—paying bills, having the carpets cleaned, work, picking up kids, soccer, football, laundry. But if you ask me to go have coffee, I'll find a way to join you. It's one of my vices.

If there's something you love to do so much that you'll

drop everything to do it, you might be able to work it to your advantage. If riding horses on Sunday afternoon gives you time with a friend to wind down and be encouraged, do it. If taking time out of your day to go for coffee refreshes you, go. But make sure you are discussing the right things.

When I steal away with my friends, we always take the time to share one another's burdens and remind each other that Christ is still in the picture—leading, holding, being the role model for our kids. Seek out those friends who won't just kill time with you but who will build you up and help you stay on course.

As iron sharpens iron, moms raising boys can help each other laugh about situations that should be laughed about and cry about situations that tear us down. Being there for each other helps us give society a little grace as it learns lessons about encouraging the individual hero, regardless of the opinions about our individual wars. Remind each other when you have coffee with a friend that with Christ in the home, your home is complete.

Now, when people ask me, "Have you found men who will serve as role models in your sons' lives?" I can smile and say that I have. It may not be what they had in mind—a Big Brother program or soccer coaches—but I do have the perfect role model *involved* in their lives. He is the Author of Fatherhood. It doesn't get more perfect than that.

And with Him, we are involved in the boys' lives every day. Society says that is the key to success for our boys—statistically speaking, that is. So when I read back over the statistics or hear someone say that my sons will be failures because they are living in a "broken" single-parent home, I can rest assured they are not talking about me at all. Not my boys. Because our home isn't broken. And our home has a Father and a role model. With Him in the picture, I *can* do this! *You* can do it well too. Join with other single moms who can look at each other over coffee and say, "It's not always easy, but I know I can raise my sons well."

1 What Makes You So Sure?
Knowing the Heavenly Father in Your Life

A father to the fatherless, a defender of widows, is God in his holy dwelling place (Ps. 68:5).

The LORD watches over the alien and sustains the fatherless and the widow, but he frustrates the ways of the wicked (Ps. 146:9).

I CERTAINLY DIDN'T FEEL PREPARED to be a single mom when it was thrust upon me. It wasn't my plan to raise children alone. When I found myself separated and consequently divorced from my sons' father, I was scared and overwhelmed. How will I do this alone? I've never been a little boy! How will I show them what it means to be a man? How will I show them how to be fathers? Will they only know how to *sit down* on the toilet? (Believe it or not, that was one of my greatest fears).

I purchased a book called *Fathering like the Father*, hoping to learn what a good father would do so I could do some of those things. I also bought Dr. Dobson's book, *Bringing up Boys*, hoping to understand my foreign little creatures. In fact, I bought every book I could get my hands on; but they seemed to raise more questions than they answered. All of them emphasized how critical it is to have a father in the home. The books seemed to suggest that without a man in the house, I was pretty much doomed.

> I decided to hold tight to the promise that God the Father is the perfect Father who will be the head of our home and father to my boys.

I finally decided that the books on the market each have one or two good nuggets to learn from, but for the most part, you can just throw them away. The only book with real answers is the Bible. While society constantly teaches just the opposite, I decided to hold tight to the promise that God the Father is the perfect Father who will be the head of our home and father to my boys. Together we would do it. What better partner to have than the one who is completely perfect in every way?

I am constantly asked how I'm managing to raise two boys on my own. I struggle with an answer. The one thing that gives me comfort and encourages me that I can do it is because the Bible tells me so. I read it as if God wrote a personal letter to me to tell me that He will be there for me. When the God of all creation tells you that you can do it, you better believe it!

You may not yet know the Heavenly Father, and that's OK. The stories in the Bible, however, are universal, and anyone who is raising boys will be able to relate to the experiences and concepts and find them helpful. "But as for me and my household, we will serve the LORD" (Josh. 24:15). I guess the answer to the often asked question of how I do it is simply that I could NOT do it without the Father as the head of our home. If you don't know Him, I hope you will meet Him.

The Plan

During the years I worked with women and girls who were experiencing unplanned pregnancies, I learned quickly that the initial shock of testing positive for pregnancy overrides whatever else is said to them at that moment. They are in such a state of confusion they rarely hear or remember anything said. They are completely preoccupied with the revelation of their new circumstance. Suddenly, they must decide whether or not to choose life for their child, figure out if they can care for a baby, determine who they must tell. It is a lot to take in. My first suggestion was always that they take some time to digest the information.

I always asked them to commit to writing down three things they would accomplish before the next meeting in one week. Just three things. That's it. The three things could consist of simple things such as taking prenatal vitamins. What those women needed was the sense of accomplishment that comes from feeling they were making progress on this overwhelming new direction of their lives. Rather than becoming discouraged and giving up, it helped give them something positive to do and kept them processing and returning for the next steps to take until they could get their feet back under them and start moving again. It's a good practice whenever life gets overwhelming. Just break it down into manageable pieces. It's a tool I use every day. I like lists; they are manageable. And at the end of a long day they help me see that I really have accomplished something—even if it's something as simple as helping another mom over coffee.

The Confusion

I think confusion comes when we concentrate on *proving* we can raise sons on our own rather than focusing on taking the steps toward actually *doing* it. That's one of the many reasons I'm so sure God is in the picture. Because society and the world want us to perform in order to prove to them that we can be as good as two people. But God wants us to thrive, to be fulfilled, and to point our sons toward Him on a daily basis to receive the leadership and fathering they need. I know this, because He wants all of us—men, women, and children—to look to Him for guidance every day.

> He wants all of us—men, women, and children—to look to Him for guidance every day.

I've heard it said that the Lord allows us to fall down so we are forced to look up, meaning that when we humans finally exhaust all our own resources, we often then try to find God. Personally, I would rather try to find God a little sooner and avoid enduring all the trials and pain that finally cause me to turn to Him! Maybe you've already discovered through grief that you need God to comfort you. Or maybe you've discovered through financial trials that you need God's provision. The Bible says "I can do every-thing through Him who gives me strength" (Phil. 4:13).

Society's reaction to that verse sometimes seems to tell us, "I can do all things through Christ, except raise a son without a father, because statistics tell us that we really need a man to do that." No, the Bible says *all* things—*all*. So no matter what circumstance has brought you to the place of raising sons alone, you can look to Him for the strength to do it well.

The Marriage Debate

Recently I asked a good friend what she thought about what society drums into single moms raising sons and what her response is. How did she raise such great boys on her own?

Cathy's husband was put in jail when her boys were 2 and 4 years old. They are now 16 and 18, and they are awe-some young men! She has done a great job with them. They are independent, they both love the Lord, and they are already successful with their own start-up company. They teach abstinence education to youth in schools, lead worship, and have their own band they named "Not4Got-ten." Their slogan is "Be the voice, not the echo." I adore these two young men.

While at dinner with Cathy and her boys, I asked her what she thought of all the rhetoric about single moms raising failures. She agreed that the hype was hurtful to her, because she felt it was an attack on her sons. She was NOT what the statistics claimed she was, and she is confident she is raising wonderful men. She simply said, "Ask Blake what he says first when he speaks about abstinence and self esteem to high school students."

So I turned to Blake and asked him. He said, "I hear all the time that boys in single-parent homes will grow up to be failures and rebel, even end up in jail. So I decided if they all think I am going to rebel, I'll rebel against their stereotype. I'm not going to be a failure—I'm rebelling against *that.*"

These two boys had a father with skin on whom they spoke to every night by phone who also pointed them to the Heavenly Father. But more importantly, both boys stayed focused on the Heavenly Father as evidenced by everything they did—right down to their band.

Generations of Success

Cathy is a mom raising successful men. When I look at my boys and Cathy's boys, I see that they are not failures. I speak to adult male friends who are successful, happily married men today, and many of them came from single-parent homes. How? Is this single-mom household a new phenomenon?

I found some interesting statistics supporting the fact that this is not new. During the Depression, men were leaving their wives and kids at a rate that outpaces today's divorce rate. However, I think the political argument of that was different. I don't think single parenting was the issue that was considered the "downfall" of the day. I think they understood it was economics.

War? That has been around since Cane and Abel. During the Revolutionary War, John Adams was away fighting for eight years. He left his wife and five kids behind with no child support, no government assistance, no Medicaid, and no weekend visits to give her a break or model how to be a man to their young sons, one of which grew up to be President.

Abigail Adams was a strong Christian woman who single-handedly led her family in the face of great adversity. There was a war going on in her backyard—literally. She managed to be a teacher, provider, mother, held down full-time work to feed her family, and raised successful Christian men. She knew the Lord was her provider while her husband was gone as evidenced in her letters to her husband and their friends.

Statistics Dispelled

I've seen research sited that says boys raised in single parent homes are more likely to be homosexual. Some research says boys raised without fathers will be more aggressive and given to being bullies. Yet another researcher just came out with a new book on "maverick moms" that says boys raised by moms will turn out as some sort of super-males because they absorb the better characteristics of womanhood and bring those characteristics to their lives as men.

I find these extremes absurd. Could it be that the bullies grew up to be bullies because of abuse or fighting in the home? I'm sure many boys do have pent-up aggression. But is the only contributing factor the lack of a male presence? What about the *quality* of male presence? In fact, there is a study that says it is not the kids of single moms who are the most dysfunctional; the kids became dysfunctional when the parents were still married. If you trace those kids of single parents back to their dysfunctional origin, it was the fighting and other factors that resulted in a single-mom home with a dysfunctional kid.

And how about the theory that boys raised by women turn out *better?* The study says these boys use their verbal skills more effectively, are more sensitive, and more in touch with their own feelings. That implies two things; that men do not naturally have characteristics that are as good as the characteristics women have (that's an extreme turn around) and it is almost an admission that boys raised by women will turn out to be more "girly."

Wow. OK—I'm either going to raise overly aggressive boys or overly sensitive boys. These seem to me to be questions of outcome, not process. It is very hard to pinpoint which factor is the *most* influential, not the *only* factor.

Head of the Home

I have a plaque in my entryway that reads:

"Christ is the Head of this home, the unseen guest at every meal, the silent listener to every conversation."

It's the first thing you see when you enter my home, and the last thing you see as you leave. It's a reminder to me to walk with Christ every day, and it is evident to all who enter my home. Christ is real, not just a billowy figment of imagination. He is sitting with us at meals, visiting with us as a family, leading decisions, and participating in daily life.

I think this concept was planted during my growing-up years when my mom reminded me to behave as if Jesus was sitting right next to me when I was in public or on a date because He is always with us! That image was deeply embedded. When I went to kiss a guy, Jesus was sitting right next to me. Would He approve of my behavior with this guy?

This was before the "What Would Jesus Do?" craze. Before WWJD, there was "Jesus is sitting next to you. Behave yourself!"

I'm not suggesting that fear should be the only motivating factor in how to live a good life. But I am suggesting that to raise successful sons, just taking them to church on Sunday won't be enough. They need to see you living your own life as if God is in control, and then they will model what they see in you. You must show them that Jesus is involved in every decision in your life if you want them to live the same way. And if you haven't been living that way up to this point and haven't taken an interest in whether or not your sons are living that way, it is never too late to start!

Prove It to Them

We were house hunting, trying to find the perfect house a little further out in the country. Every time we found what my oldest son thought was the perfect house, we were either outbid or I felt we needed to wait to make a decision, and then we would lose the house to another buyer. My son was getting frustrated. All he saw was that I was keeping him from getting his perfect house. But I kept telling him, "God is in control. He is leading this family and this decision. If we don't get this house, it's because it's not the one He wants for us."

We found another perfect house. My son was even more adamant that this house was *the* house. But it was $100,000 more than we could afford. So I said to my son again, "If that really is the perfect one—the one God wants us to have—then they will lower the price and offer us the house." Of course, my teenage son was very upset because he thought I was being foolish! "That will never happen, Mom! You're going to lose this house too!" But I remained firm. We were going to wait, pray, and see what God did.

> If you show them how God is leading in your everyday life, they won't have to experience tragedy to recognize their need for the Lord.

One afternoon as we were leaving our house to do errands, the owners of that perfect house came walking up my driveway. They came to me to ask if I was still interested in their house and if I would buy it for $100,000 less than their original asking price. Of course, we took the house. When my son and I got in the car to leave to do our errands, he very solemnly said, "Wow, Mom. You were right; God did it!"

Yes, God did it. And He has done it again and again. But you have to be willing to say up front—again and again—"We are going to wait on the Lord." Then be willing to do the waiting. God is not always going to grant you three wishes. But again, if you wait on the Lord, He will give you the desires of your heart. And you need to point that out to your boys all along the way so they will have the opportunity to witness God taking care of things firsthand. If you show them how God is leading in your everyday life, my hope is that they won't have to experience greater tragedy than they already have to recognize their need for dependence on the Lord.

This house was exactly how I would have designed it—right down to the white color and the light-colored wood. I have a binder full of pictures of my "dream house," and that is what the inside of my house looks like. I pointed that out to my sons. God didn't just answer our prayers and provide a house for us; He knew the desires of my heart and provided them. God cares about the littlest details.

Don't Forget to Ask Him

I want my sons to learn to turn to God through the experiences we share together. I'm afraid I didn't learn my lesson so gently. My husband and I got married because I was pregnant with our first son. I had just graduated from college and was on my way to graduate school when I met him. He was a good-looking guy, but we had nothing in common. I broke up with him because we were arguing a lot, but then found out I was pregnant. I was in such shock from the circumstances; I immediately went into "fix-it" mode. I decided the best thing to do was marry him so the baby would have a father. I reasoned that I was a capable person and I could handle everything else.

We got married, but the relationship quickly deteriorated into complete dysfunction. I went to counseling on my own—thinking it was best for the boys if we stayed together. At this point there was a second child in the picture. One night, my four-year-old was awakened by our fighting. I will never forget the look on his face when he toddled into our room when he heard us fighting and said, "Wrestle with me, Daddy, not Mommy."

That is the split second I realized that what I was doing was not right for my boys. I didn't want them raised thinking abusive behavior was all right. It was scary to venture out on my own with a newborn and a four-year-old. But I went before God and surrendered everything, saying, *Lord, there is no way in the world I can do this alone. I need you.*

Through the many nights of crying desperation, I reflected on the past five years. What had gone wrong? Why couldn't I make it work? I really *am* a strong person. Anyone who knows me would agree. Many would say I'm too strong. But I failed. Not at the marriage—although that was one loss and failure I was faced with. But my real failure was in thinking I could fix it my way when faced with a crisis pregnancy. I had great plans to make it all better, fix the situation and the sin. But they were all worthless because I forgot the first step. I forgot to ask God what He wanted me to do.

God's plans are always perfect. And although they don't make sense at first, they are always better than anything I could have planned myself. This is something I knew in my life early-on. But in this major testing, I failed to simply ask Him the big question. I never got on my knees and asked Him, *What do I do now?*

I went on to work in crisis pregnancy centers—which proves that God can use our mistakes and hurts to His glory in helping others in ways we can't foresee. And knowing what I know now, I'm sure had I asked God, He would have given me any number of different directions other than marrying a man who was physically abusive to me and the boys and given to infidelity.

Hitting bottom before you are ready to look up is a good description of me. There was no way in the world it looked possible at that point to raise two small boys alone. I hear the same from moms everywhere. The realization that you are responsible for raising sons can be an eye-opening experience.

Quantity and Quality

I am in awe of a friend of mine for the way she handled this realization. Ann has been divorced for 14 years, which is not uncommon. Her husband was caught cheating on her, and he married that gal after Ann's divorce. That is not uncommon either. What is so amazing about Ann is that at the time of the divorce, she had nine children ranging from 8 months to 13 years in age, four of which were boys.

Ann recalls that when she was faced with the unthinkable, she held tightly to her faith to get her through. That certainly makes sense. It is recorded that survivors of tragedies—the Holocaust to name one—survived because of their faith. Now I'm not saying raising nine kids alone is a crisis equal to the magnitude of the Holocaust, but I'm sure there were days when it felt close to that for Ann!

With tragedy such as divorce and abandonment, or death of a spouse, it is tempting to blame God and be bitter or angry. And those are all real feelings that are justified. The good news is that God is a big God who can handle your anger when life throws you a curve. Even David in the Bible was an extremely emotional guy, and he cried out to the Lord in anguish. And David was referred to as the "man after God's own heart." That's quite an honor. If David got mad at God and he was still honored that way, I think God can handle just about anything you can throw at Him.

Knight in Shining Armor

Part of me hesitates, however. It's true that David made big mistakes and still had the character to admit it and change his ways. And that is something I want my boys to do. But how did he come to the point in his life that he was willing and able to place his whole life in God's hands? I think for us, it's coming to the point where we must rely on God and then see God really come through for us. As He comes through for us again and again, we learn to trust that He will do it next time.

Be sure to share it with your boys when God comes through for you and for them so they won't have to learn it on bigger and more painful things later—all by themselves. We women try to "fix" things, and we think we can fix the lack of a man in the house with a man. *If only I had a husband, everything would be just right.* Or, *If I can fix this man I've got, everything will be great!* Unfortunately, that thinking is just a distraction from the real solution—which is looking to God in the first place.

As has happened to me a lot, I picked up a book that changed my way of thinking just when I needed it. The book was *Knight in Shining Armor*. In this book, the author suggests making the Lord the "Prince" in my fairytale, rather than expecting a man to come to my rescue.

We tend to expect a man to be our protector, our lover, our romantic pursuit. But in order to be whole enough to offer ourselves to someone, we need to focus our energy on making the Lord our pursuit—to spend as much time thinking about the Lord as we would a new romantic interest. We need to give God first place in our lives, and then we will be whole enough to offer a whole person to a relationship with a man as well as being there for our kids. If we make God first in our lives, then He, if He chooses, can put a man in our lives who will be those things for us. But it will be because of Him, not because of who that man with skin on is.

If you learn to trust and rely on God completely—even when things look hopeless—He will amaze you every time.

We have heard all our lives that God should come first. But to put that into practical action is difficult. A human man is something you can touch, see, and hear. It takes a little more practice to hear and see the Lord. But I decided to make a real effort to put Him as the head of my home in practical ways and to make Him first in my life.

If you learn to trust and rely on God completely—even when things look hopeless—He will amaze you every time. The outcome may not be the outcome you pictured or how you would have done it yourself, but in the end it will work out better than you could have hoped for. I'm a slow learner sometimes, but I have learned to ask God first and to let Him go before me in all matters. He is an excellent decision maker. He has a better overall picture of the situation than I do anyway!

Fragrance of Life

Remember my friend Cathy, whose husband is in prison? Both she and her husband have a ministry to families in prison. Her hope and faith in the Lord—even in the face of injustice and adversity—is a constant encouragement to me. We share often, and do not get nearly enough time drinking coffee together because she lives so far away in Ohio, but she wrote this in a letter to me once and gave me permission to share it with you.

I remember a time when I found myself standing over Brandon in the intensive care unit. He had had a severe allergic reaction to something and was struggling to breathe. He was so sound asleep (or sedated) that he did not even respond when the nursing staff administered his care. I sat for hours by his bed just watching him sleep and praying fervently that God would restore him to complete health. I felt abandoned and alone and completely ill-equipped to deal with this situation. Since sleeping in the hospital room was not allowed, the nurses finally convinced me to rest in the parents' lounge while he slept, promising to come and get me at any change in his condition or if he awakened. I slept for about 40 minutes before I found myself walking back through the glass doors into the pediatric intensive care unit. They insisted he did not even know if I was there or not, so I may as well take advantage of the opportunity to get some rest. I had to see him. I quietly walked into his room, pushing the curtain aside as I approached his bed. He moaned softly and said, "Mommy? Mommy is that you?"

"Yes, baby, Mommy is here. How did you know it was me?"

Much to my surprise, he replied, "I could smell you."

I wondered if I should even ask the next question, but I did. "What do I smell like, Brandon?"

"Like a hug," he whispered.

God began to speak of His faithfulness to us. Through Brandon's observation about the aroma of a hug, God showed me that all I do and think affects my children. They will know the best of me and the worst of me. The things that are not appealing (sins) are those things in my life that will leave an unpleasant aroma behind and infect my sons with the sickness of this world. The sweet smelling parts of my life are nothing less than God manifesting in me to reassure, comfort, protect, and heal my sons. He was gently telling me I could truly choose to "do it alone" and risk raising my sons infected with the stench of the world and the disgusting odor of being raised fatherless or I could choose to allow Him to work in me and through me to protect them and nurture them by filling them with the sweet perfume of His constant presence in their lives. It is the sweet fragrance of His abiding presence, undying love, and unwavering fathering that raises boys to become men of unwavering essence."

Cathy wrote that to me without ever seeing my writing in this book. That's how I know we are on the right track. Without conferring, we have arrived at the same conclusions. It is our decision to make God the head of our home and raise men after God's own heart. We have decided through our experiences that to go the way of the world would be to give in to the doomsday statistics of society and fail. He has a better plan for us if we choose to take it.

Coffee with a Friend

Things to Remember:

- With the Heavenly Father in the picture, the family is not broken.

- Society is wrong—moms CAN do it and HAVE been doing it for centuries.

- Your boys will turn out great! Others have done it, and you can too!

- He promises to be the husband to the widow, our Knight in Shining Armor.

- Little eyes are watching us, lead by example.

- Knowing Christ as Savior is the key to success. If you haven't done so already, invite Him into your life and to be the head of your home.

Meeting the Author of Fatherhood

Some people wonder why it's important to know the Author of Fatherhood. Maybe they have had a bad experience with men in their lives—or even with their own fathers—and God is the last thing they think they need.

Some may even think a woman can't be a Christian and be a single mom or have any other flaws in her life, because only good people or married people can attain a perfect Christian life.

The other night I was at a friend's house for the most amazing luau in her backyard. She started talking about another friend of hers who had not come, and she thought the reason was because this person was a Christian and wouldn't approve because there were hula dancers. Then she realized I was in the group she was talking to, and she recovered with, "Except you, Dana. You're a cool Christian. You're not stuffy—you know, like most Christians." I laughed, but it dawned on me that many people have a stereotypical idea of what it means to be a Christian, and it doesn't include moms raising boys, broken marriages, or what they consider to be "cool" people.

But, I can assure you, I am very cool, I am a single mom, and I am a Christian.

At church I occasionally see Kristina, a single mom

who is raising one son. Recently she told me all that was going on with her son—the disappointments of Father's Day and her 9-year-old son trying to reach out to his father only to be rejected again. It breaks her heart. I know exactly what she is talking about, having walked through it just a few years ago. I asked her if she had reminded her son of his Heavenly Father who never ignores him or lets him down.

> Sometimes we know Christ as Savior, but we forget to lean on Him in a real and personal way.

She said, "You know, I know that and all, but I guess I just forget sometimes."

Sometimes it's not a case of *refusing* to have a relationship with God. Sometimes we know Christ as Savior, but we forget to lean on Him in a real and personal way. That's why it's important to not only meet Him but also to build a relationship with Him. And building a relationship with Him—like all relationships—takes a little work. But it is so worth it.

There are two important reasons I need to know the Author of Fatherhood—for me and for my sons. For me, because I simply cannot do this huge task alone. I know I have family and friends and a church family, but to supply my real needs and provide for me and the boys, a supernatural touch is required. When I do my taxes at the end of each year and look at the total income I have brought in and all the amazing things my sons and I have done and places we have visited, it is nothing short of a miracle that we get by, let alone thrive! And when I list all the things I accomplish each day and each year, I create another to-do list of goals for me and the boys. Again, it is nothing short of a miracle that God allows me to work full time, take care of kids, scrapbook, go on vacation, write books, write for the local paper and Christian papers, take care of two horses, three dogs, two birds, and two gold fish (that just keep living). Plus, laundry that is always waiting, bills that are always there, cleaning house, keeping up the yard, being the team mom for both soccer and football, traveling for work, volunteering at my church. Really—how could a person do it without God regularly working miracles? I need Him.

I need Him because Christ is hope, and without Him, my life would simply be too overwhelming. Remember I told you that the first thing to do in crisis is to ask Him what you should do? Still, people don't think to ask Him until they have no other choice. They've tried everything and it isn't working, so they figure they might as well give God a try as a last resort.

Let me save you a little time. If you are a mom raising sons—in *any* circumstance—it won't work without God. Jesus said, "I have come that they may have life, and have it to the full" (John 10:10).

So How Do You Meet Him?

First, remember that the first move was His. God loves you and your kids more than you can imagine, and He wants to have a personal relationship with you. He is already pursuing a relationship with you.

For God so loved the world, that He gave His only begotten Son, that whoever believes in Him should not perish, but have eternal life (John 3:16, NASV).

Now this is eternal life, that they may know You, the only true God and Jesus Christ whom You have sent (John 17:3).

So why is it that some people do not have a personal relationship with God? Because our sin cuts us off from God so we cannot have a personal relationship with Him and experience His love.

For all have sinned and fall short of the glory of God (Rom. 3:23, NASV).

Notice that the Bible says *all* have sinned. It does not say, "Single moms have sinned, and so fall short of the glory of God, and their kids must pay the price of her mistakes for the rest of their lives." It does not say, "Those whose marriages have failed have sinned and those who are married are all good." It says *all* have sinned—married, single, man, woman, everyone has sinned and fallen short.

When I work with girls facing crisis pregnancies, they often face shame and embarrassment. I tell them the difference between their sin and the sins of the people they see at the mall is that the consequence of their sin is visible. But all sin is created equal, and whether it is visible or not, it keeps us from relationship with God.

"The wages of sin is death (spiritual separation from God)" (Rom. 6:23).

God is holy and pure and perfect, and before we have a personal relationship with Him, we are cut off from Him because He cannot tolerate sin. People often try to find a full and meaningful life through their own efforts.

This past summer I decided to take a drive with the boys to Arizona to see the Grand Canyon. It seemed like a great idea, but actually doing it was another thing. I'm afraid of heights. Actually, I've been skydiving and that wasn't a problem, so, I think I am not afraid of heights as much as I am afraid of edges. Let me tell you, the Grand Canyon is just one big, gigantic, scary edge!

While I was standing (a few feet back) on the edge of the Grand Canyon, I said to the boys, "How far do you think we could get if we took a running jump toward the North Rim?"

It is physically impossible to do anything on our own to bridge the gap between us and perfection.

I was trying to give them a picture of what the Bible means when it says we have all fallen short. It is physically impossible to do anything on our own to bridge the gap between us and perfection. But the Bible clearly teaches that there is one way to bridge this gap.

Jesus Christ is God's only cure for our sin. Through Him, you can know God personally and experience His love. God doesn't want us to be separated from Him. We were all created to have a personal relationship with God, but then sin got in the way. Jesus died in our place, and He rose again from the dead and is our only way to bridge the gap.

But God demonstrates His own love toward us, in that while we were yet sinners, Christ died for us (Rom. 5:8, NASV).

"I am the way, and the truth, and the life; no one comes to the Father, but through Me" (John 14:6, NASV).

God has done the work to bridge the gap that cuts us off from Him. He sent His Son, Jesus Christ, to die on the cross in our place to pay the penalty for our sin. But it is not enough just to know these truths. People who just know that Jesus is real won't be any more saved than Satan himself. Even Satan knows God exists. But to be saved we must take the next step and "cross the bridge." We must individually receive Jesus Christ as Savior and Lord; then we can know God personally and experience His love.

"But as many as received Him, to them He gave the right to become children of God, even to those who believe in His name" (John 1:12, NASV).

We receive Christ by personal invitation when we acknowledge that we are sinful and bridge that gap the size of the Grand Canyon by asking God to forgive us and come into our lives and change us. To ask for forgiveness and repent of our sin simply means to turn and go in another direction. Once Christ comes into our lives and forgives our sins, we can begin a personal relationship with Him. We receive Jesus Christ by faith, as an act of the will.

You can meet Him and ask Him into your heart right now. God is not as concerned with you saying the right words as He is with the attitude of your heart. And remember, God wants a relationship with all people—especially you. There is nothing in your past, no sin so great, that God can't forgive and heal you.

There is no one so bad nor anyone so good that his or her life won't be improved by the presence of Christ. But, remember the instructions we receive on planes?

We're instructed to place the oxygen mask on ourselves before placing it on someone else. In the same way, you and I must accept His love for us before we can help our children know His love for them.

Here is a suggested prayer to help you express your trust in Jesus:

Dear Lord Jesus, I want to know you personally. Thank you for dying on the cross for my sins and for rising from the dead. I receive you as my Savior and Lord. I trust you now to forgive my sins and give me eternal life. Please lead me to become the kind of person you want me to be. Amen.

2 Boys Need a Father
Knowing the Heavenly Father in Their Lives

SHORTLY AFTER MY HUSBAND LEFT OUR HOME, I found myself in a Sunday School class full of singles, which included men. Men were not my favorite creatures for a while, and on this particular Sunday, the lesson was on David—and Bathsheba.

David had an affair with Bathsheba, had her husband killed in battle so he could marry her, was such a horrible father that his sons rebelled, and in general, just messed up and hurt people. At the time, I was more interested in focusing on my own pain rather than any faults I might have, so it was just fine with me to discuss all the ways this man had blown it.

Then the teacher said the unthinkable. "The Bible calls David a 'man after God's own heart.' He is the only man spoken of so highly in the entire Bible!" *What? Are you kidding me?* What is God thinking?

I decided to learn more about David and why he was called a man after God's own heart. Charles Swindoll had written a series of books on Bible characters, so I picked up his book *David: A Man of Passion and Destiny* that day.

I learned that David was actually a man of character. When he did something wrong, he was willing to admit it and ask for forgiveness. He mourned his own sons and the poor decisions he made with his family. He tried to rectify them—even to the point of his own loss. And David learned that relying on God was *always* better than anything he might plan or carry out on his own.

My favorite story is when David had been wronged by a man named Nabal that the Bible describes as "surly" and "mean in his dealings." He was dishonest and was not willing to give David his due. In fact, his name actually means "fool," which in the scriptures doesn't mean he was stupid —it is a person who says, "There is no God." David took 400 men to kill Nabal, but he was persuaded by Nabal's wife not to kill him.

David could easily have killed him that night. He had an opportunity, the army at his door. But David decided to honor the request and leave vengeance to the Lord. God had a plan, and David decided to obey God and follow His plan. It turned out far better than if David had taken matters into his own hands. In fact, the Bible says of Nabal that the next day "his heart died within him so that he became as a stone. About ten days later, the LORD struck Nabal and he died" (1 Sam. 25:37). Nabal just up and died and David never had to sin and murder him.

After reading about David, I came to respect all that God was trying to teach us in the "man after God's own heart." I bought a copy of the book for my oldest son and the Bible study workbook that goes with it. It's really an action-packed story—slaying giants, shepherd to king, betrayal, David's friendship with Jonathan. Even my son, who doesn't like to read much, read it pretty quickly.

Male Bashing Future Fathers

During the time I was angry with men in general, I was talking to a friend on the phone, and I was telling her how horrible men were—making a joke about what stupid, uncaring liars and cheaters they were. When I got off the phone, my son—about five at the time—looked up at me and said, "I'm one of those, right?" I was crushed.

What a fool I was! Of course my precious sons are one of "those," and I was making them out to be evil monsters! Men are not evil monsters, and I needed to get my head on straight pronto if I was going to raise my sons to be *good* strong men. Someday they are going to be husbands and fathers. I realized my need to focus on equipping them to be the best husbands and fathers they could be instead of dwelling on my unfortunate experience and blaming the entire male population. These two boys are the ones God put in my care to nurture and love as they grow up to become fathers themselves.

We All Long for One

There is a reason we seek father figures in our lives; it's in our nature. God created us in His image, and He is

God the Father, God the Son, and God the Holy Spirit. While society teaches us we need a man with skin on to make us happy, the truth is that what is lacking in our lives cannot be filled by any human.

The reality is that earthly fathers are sometimes good and sometimes bad. But the original is always perfect.

Sometimes we get it backwards. Our experience with fathers on earth gives us an improper picture of who God really is. The reality is that earthly fathers are sometimes good and sometimes bad. But the original is always perfect. Instead of measuring fathers against other fathers, we should be measuring fathers to God, who is the original Author of Fatherhood. No human father (or mother for that matter) is always an accurate reflection of God the Father.

A young friend of mine who is raising her two-year-old son alone was asked by her son one day, "Why don't I have a father?"

That's a tough question, and if we are not prepared, it can catch us off guard. Our gut reaction may be to put down the father or men in general. It might make us feel defensive. But it's critical that we have an answer that addresses the child's needs and fills the hole in his heart. We can do that by pointing him to the only Father who is always there for all of us. I was not ready when my own son had a meltdown.

Father's Day

My two sons and I always found the days before Father's Day difficult. Living just a few miles from our home, their father often made arrangements to come see the boys, but would then fail to show up and leave them waiting on the front porch. My oldest, seven-year-old CJ, would wait until it got dark. If you have experienced this, you know there is no greater pain in the world. It broke my heart every time it happened, and it crushed his spirit. I tried every trick in the book, including not telling him his father was coming so he wouldn't be disappointed if he didn't show, and would be pleasantly surprised if he did. But his father would tell him and make big promises and still not show up. My instinct was to protect my sons at all costs, but I seemed to be powerless to keep this pain from them.

One day as we drove home from shopping, the boys were playing in the car with the toys they'd bought. When CJ dropped a piece to his game between the seats, he stared out the window, and his lip began to quiver. I pulled off the road, crawled into the back seat, and held him as he sobbed. CJ was a strong little guy. He rarely told me how he felt. He just kept things bottled up inside until they spilled out. I tried not to push him but waited for those moments when he was ready to share his hurts with me.

As Father's Day approached, every store sign and Hallmark commercial was a painful reminder of our situation. CJ never mentioned it, but I could see the pain in his eyes. Nathan was only three, and CJ was in school. In class they were making Father's Day crafts. CJ never wanted to show his hurt, so he never told the teacher that he didn't have a father involved in his life to give the gifts to. In years past, he just quietly made the presents at school and then sneaked them home and hid them in his closet. I had asked him if he wanted to give the Father's Day presents to me or his uncle or Grandpa. But talking about it at all was painful, and he just wanted to do what he was told to do in class and then hide the gifts or throw them away when I wasn't looking.

So this particular year, I decided we needed to get our minds off of the constant reminder. His tears were getting closer to the surface as Father's Day approached, and any little thing caused him to cry. So we decided to spend Father's Day at Disneyland with some friends. Because we would miss church on Sunday morning, we attended the night before. Nathan went to the preschool class and CJ went to "big church" with me. During worship service, CJ started to cry again. I hadn't thought about church that week being all about fathers!

He held back the tears as best he could. But when the

> "Let's spend every Father's Day celebrating the dad you're going to be someday."

pastor asked all the fathers to stand so he could honor them, his tears gushed.

We walked out into the foyer where I put my arms around him. A pastor offered to pray with us in an empty office. There were a few people around, but there wasn't anything they could do, so we retreated to the pastor's office where we could cry and I could hold him in private. Despite CJ's many sessions of counseling, he said, "How come Daddy doesn't want to see me? Why did he leave us?"

I cried with him, then we talked. "CJ, you know you have a Father who really loves you. You know that? He loves you so much, He would die for you! He will never leave you or let you down. Never. I have an idea," I said. "Let's spend every Father's Day celebrating the dad you're going to be someday. You'll get presents and cards for maybe 15 years before you're even a dad!" He liked that idea and began to dry his eyes.

We discussed some of the Heavenly Father's qualities he wanted to emulate for his children. CJ named the first two on his list: reading the Bible and teaching his children to pray. So as CJ's first Father's Day gift, I gave him a dad's devotional Bible in black leather with his name printed in gold. We started laughing about all the things he was going to do with his kids and the great dad he was going to be. We shifted the focus from what he didn't have to all he does have and is going to have. I remember being up late running all over town finding the Bible that night so he would have it right away. Luckily, I knew someone who worked at the Bible bookstore and could get one for me. CJ and I were able to work on it together that night—writing in it.

The next morning when my alarm went off at 5:45 to get ready for Disneyland, I found my son awake and reading his Bible. CJ still missed his dad, but he had found a new focus. He discovered more than just knowing God as a good Father. He's learning to apply godly qualities to his life as well. He had listed "guidance" as one of the things a good father should give. Now he's experienced Fatherly guidance firsthand.

That day, on our way to the Pirates of the Caribbean, I leaned over and whispered to CJ, "Happy Father's Day." He smiled, then ran off to get in line just like any seven-year-old.

I remember the words I wrote inside his Bible:

Starting this year, Father's Day will become a time to celebrate you and the father you will one day become. You'll get a Father's Day gift (this Bible being the first), but each year, you will list another attribute of God to pass on to your children.

Son, you'll not understand the kind of deep love Christ has for us until you have kids of your own. By then, you will have filled these pages and know what it means to put love into action.

God bless you my little man. I love you, Mom.

Years later, this story has been shared with teachers, friends, *Single Parent Magazine*, and through the Internet. Single moms and married women have written me to tell me how much this has touched their lives. Single parenting touches everyone in one way or another—whether you've experienced it or you are trying to help others who are experiencing it. As one woman wrote, "I am happily married, but I cried when I read this because my husband comes from a broken home, and I was so touched by this for him." It still brings tears to my eyes thinking about it— for the pain of my son during that time, but also for the overwhelming opportunity God allowed us to peer into His love for us.

You would be surprised how many single-parent homes there are in your kids' classes at school. Feel free to support those moms you don't know by sharing this story with the teachers and class moms so they can love on the kids when it's time to make Father's Day gifts each June. You can download and print a copy of this story at www .forwomen.org.

Since I first wrote this, the boys have received drills, power tools, punching bags, a weight set, and my younger son has his own Father's Day Bible that we write in each year. The pages are getting full of the most incredible insights! The most important thing is to find a way to celebrate who they are and who Christ is in their lives—all the ways He is providing and has provided for them. Now Father's Day is something my boys actually look forward to— no tears in sight!

Bread and Butter

Just as it is difficult for my boys to deal with abandonment and the fact that their father is *choosing* to stay out of their lives, my friend Cathy's boys are dealing with the pain of having their father taken from them because he is in prison. Regardless of whether or not their father was guilty, to these boys all they care about is being with their father. Even I get angry because I am powerless to give my own sons their father; I can't *make* him wake up and do the right thing. But Cathy's husband wants to be with his kids and cannot. Little boys are concrete thinkers, and it's hard for them to get their young minds around abstract thoughts sometimes. But just when we least expect it, they come up with the most amazing insights.

Cathy once shared what Blake had learned about forgiveness.

"Blake missed his father terribly. His dad had been in prison for ten years and was finally scheduled to be reviewed by the parole board. Blake felt he needed his dad home more than anything else in his life. He believed with all his heart that his dad was innocent of the crimes he was convicted of. Unfortunately, his grandmother disagreed and actively fought to keep his father in prison. Time after time, Blake watched as motions were denied and appeals lost. His grandmother consistently attended hearings in opposition to his father's release and politically fought to keep his case from being overturned.

As the hearing approached, Blake decided God was telling him he had to share his feelings of anger and hurt with his grandmother. He met with her and shared all of his feelings and then asked her to *please* stop fighting and just let the courts decide his father's future and to begin by not attending the upcoming hearing. Much to his surprise, she agreed. However, on the day of the hearing, Blake watched as his grandmother walked into the courtroom to oppose his father's release.

I watched all the color drain out of Blake's face. He leaned forward, staring at his grandmother, seemingly daring her—maybe begging her—to look him in the eye. She refused to meet his eyes. Later that evening, Blake stormed to his room declaring he completely disowned his grandma and that he would never again speak to her nor agree to see her as long as he lived. I wept for the pain of seeing my son so wounded and cried out to God to somehow heal the deep wounds I knew were in Blake's heart and spirit.

Later that night, Blake woke me up. "Mom, I have to talk to you. I was telling God I was done. I was tired of being hurt, lied to, overlooked, and ignored. He let me throw a big temper tantrum before He asked me one question: *Blake, do you want to be bread or butter?* He told me I have two choices, I can choose to be bread or I can choose butter. He is letting me decide. If I choose to be bread, He showed me what would happen. When bread is left out, it either gets hard and crumbles when the least bit of pressure is rubbed against it or disintegrates if it gets wet and disappears—leaving no trace behind. If I choose butter, He showed me what that would mean. When butter is left out and melts, it can soften the hardest bread, won't dissolve in water, but leaves a mark on whatever it touches. He is asking me to be butter for Grandma. To let Him use me and my life to soften Grandma's heart toward Him and to impact others for His glory. It is so hard, but I know I have to be butter. In order to be butter, I have to forgive her." I sat and cried with my son as he wept in my arms. Knowing I also had to make a choice; I made my decision to let God use me as butter. It was one of many times God spoke as the loving Father to His sons and then used my sons to teach me."

Cathy had to start that relationship between her sons and God the Father early in their lives, so when they got to be teenagers they had that deep relationship and could hear the Lord speaking to them. Kids learn by repetition. Start teaching them early, and often.

Although the boys do not have their dad at home with them, even their father has helped them get grounded in who the real Father of their lives is. Cathy shared another situation.

Never Forsaken

After being gone 11 years, my husband, Ron, was suddenly released from prison to come home. It was a wonderful, joyful, long awaited and prayed for day! My sons had been 2 and 4 when their father went to prison for a crime he never committed. It had been a long road filled with many opportunities for us to witness God's faithfulness in various areas of our lives. Now we had a wonderful opportunity to celebrate the beginning of a new season—and I thought the end of the season where we had to solely rely on God to be Husband and Father. My husband was home; the boys' father was finally home.

It did not take long for a confrontation between my oldest son, Blake, and his father. The second day, Ron went to sit at the table. Blake was seated at the head of the table. Ron casually told Blake that was his place and Blake could move to sit next to him. Blake insisted this was *his* place and Ron could sit next to him. Ron gently, but firmly, told Blake, "I'm home now. You get to just be the son. It's OK, Blake, I am home. I am going to take my place, and you can take your rightful place." Blake reluctantly moved, but was obviously not convinced.

Within days, another confrontation presented itself. This time, it escalated into a physical altercation. I could hear Blake yelling and heard something drop, so I ran upstairs to find Ron holding Blake tightly and Blake sobbing and yelling at the same time, "You may be my father, but I won't let you be my dad again. I know you'll leave again. Something will happen—you'll die or go back to prison or leave, and I cannot go through losing you again. So I am not letting you in! Do you hear me? You cannot be my dad because you cannot promise me you will never leave me again!" Ron held him as he quieted and then softly agreed with Blake. "You are so right, Blake. I cannot promise I will never leave you. I do not know what the future holds for either of us. But you're also wrong. I am your dad. I will always be your dad whether I am here beside you or not. God, He is your Father. He is the only one who will never leave you—never forsake you and never let you down. Trust your Father, Blake. Unimaginable as it is to me; He loves you more than I do, knows you better than I do, and will carry you when I cannot." God was teaching us that no matter how many people live in your house or what their earthly relationship to us is, His role as Father has to be recognized as the most important in every family. Little did we know how important that lesson was at that time. Six months later, the court overturned Ron's release, and he had to report back to prison. Although Blake grieved, he held fast to his Heavenly Father for comfort and overcame the second separation with his faith stronger than ever.

Coffee with a Friend

Things to Remember

- Find ways to celebrate the fathers they will be someday.

- Say it, live it, repeat.

- We all long for a father—point your sons to the perfect Author of Fatherhood.

- A man after God's own heart isn't perfect.

- Help them grieve their losses, whatever they might be.

- Make every hurt a learning encounter to show them the character of God the Father.

3 Sink or Swim
The "Train" in "Train Up a Child" Is an Action Verb

"Train a child in the way he should go and when he is old he will not turn from it" (Prov. 22:6).

Training

I am the middle of three children. My father was in the Navy and gone much of the time. When he was home, he was more of a handful for my mother than we were. He was so young, he was still growing up himself. Although today he is a different man and we are very close, when we were growing up we begged my mother to divorce him. We joke that we raised him rather than the other way around. My mom was raising three kids (one boy) and dealing with a husband who was not only nonsupportive but also a burden to care for in addition to the kids. While my mother tried to keep us in church and grounded, my father was busy setting a not-so-great example. I struggled with that reality throughout my teen years, and it affected my younger brother also. Luckily, my brother is resilient, and God really does help moms raise great boys in spite of their situations. Both my father and my brother turned out great!

My father would be the first to admit he was young and foolish, and my older sister caught the brunt of my father's lack of parenting skill. I'm not sure where my father got the brilliant idea for teaching us how to swim, but his logic was that if we absolutely had to swim to save our lives, we would figure it out. He decided on a way to "teach" my sister to swim and to test his theory. She couldn't have been more than four or five years old when he tossed her into the deep end of a friend's pool and yelled at her "Sink or swim!"

She didn't swim. After what seemed like an eternity to her, my father dived in and saved her. I imagine he was angry and throwing a fit, and my sister was frightened half to death. His experiment was a disaster. Then I came along and didn't learn to swim until I was ten or twelve when I finally taught myself with some friends. My mother didn't know how to swim, so she couldn't teach us, and she hasn't learned to this day.

> Raising boys is kind of like teaching them to swim. You can't just leave them to their own devices and hope they'll somehow figure it all out.

My dad's experiment taught us one thing: Children don't learn to swim by the sink or swim method. It requires training from someone who knows how to swim who will take the time to show them. It requires guidance. I imagine there are exceptions to the rule, and someone can tell a story of learning to swim after getting into a situation where his or her life depended on it. But it's safe to say that generally the skill must be taught or at the very least practiced with someone experienced.

Raising boys is kind of like teaching them to swim. You can't just leave them to their own devices and hope they'll somehow figure it all out. They need your help and guidance. That is your job. And if their father is absent, your job is doubly difficult. And if you don't know how to swim yourself—you simply must go somewhere and learn!

Handyman Classes

I have learned to be a "Jill of all trades." I can take apart the underside of my sink and clean out a clog. I can climb up in the attic and set traps for mice. I can use a miter saw to install trim in the kids' bedrooms—and even change the blade! Usually, my first trip is to Home Depot to get the best "how to" book.

When I was newly divorced, we had a dog that constantly broke off my sprinkler heads. When pop-up sprinklers break off, they often leave a little ring of plastic stuck down in the pipe, and you must remove that little ring before you can screw in the new sprinkler head. If this has happened to you, you know there is nothing to grab hold of to unscrew the broken piece to remove it. I was just certain there was no book to help me with this problem, and I set about figuring it out by myself.

Sometimes you can stick your finger in and if the broken piece is loose enough, just twist it right out. I've also used scissors. If you stick them in there and then open the scissors just enough, you can put pressure on the sides and twist the wedged piece out. This, however, will ruin your most precious sewing scissors as well as all of your cheap ones.

If this fails, you can dig a great big hole and get the whole sleeve of the sprinkler out and replace the whole thing. That's what I did when I had frustrated all my other options and was ready to throw out the whole yard! This also leaves a big hole that must be replaced and replanted, but it gets the broken sprinkler fixed.

After figuring many different ways to take care of the problem myself, I went to Home Depot and asked how others had solved this dilemma. And do you know that there is a special tool *just* for taking out that little broken piece of a sprinkler? And it's cheap, too! The little tool is only 69 cents, much less expensive than sewing scissors or new sod. I now have about a dozen of those little tools in my garage because I still haven't figured out how to store things where I can find them. But I haven't had to dig up my yard in a long time.

When people tell me they don't need counseling after a divorce or they don't need a small group to learn about the stages of death and grieving or that their kids don't need any help coping with these life issues, I agree with them. You can struggle through the stages of grief all by yourself without the benefit of knowing others who have gone through similar things and without knowing there are tools to help you. But in the process of figuring it out on your own, you might create big holes that must be fixed in addition to your current problems. And especially in the lives of your children, you may be creating extensive damage when all you really need to do is give them access to a few simple, helpful tools to solve the problem or at least cope with it.

The tool you need may be a counselor or a small group at church or a divorce video series or a children's workshop for healing.

We used to joke and say people who didn't seek help were either a "rock" or an "island." We prided ourselves on being able to get through anything alone. But with age comes wisdom, and now I have to ask, *Why? Why not just go get the 69-cent tool?* Save yourself the headache and heartache.

The tool you need may be a counselor or a small group at church or a divorce video series or a children's workshop for healing. These tools won't do the repairs for you, but they can make the job a little easier. Read the "how to" book. That stubborn sprinkler taught me that books can really save you a lot of time if you admit you need the help. If you don't know how to raise boys—learn! And then just do it.

Not Just a Theory

The Bible says we should "train up a child." That requires action. It doesn't say to provide food and shelter and then leave it to them to find the way. Synonyms for the word "train" are *develop, prepare,* and *educate.*

If you were going to train an athlete, you would create a schedule. You would have a plan to guide him or her to learn the rules of the game and then encourage practice until the athlete was at peak performance.

Go for the Gold

The Bible tells us to "press on toward the goal to win the prize(Phil. 3:14). In this case, the prize is raising healthy men to be great fathers after their own Father's heart. You are the trainer for your son. That is what being involved is all about. That is what changes the statistical outcome for your sons.

But you are not a father, so how can you model one? I did a little research on the Internet, and did you know that most of our great composers throughout history did not have parents that were composers? Or did you know that most Olympic athletes do not have parents who are former Olympians? You don't have to be a champion to raise a champion. It is not a requirement. Athletes and musicians learn from those who can teach them what they need to know.

You don't have to be a father to raise a father. But you will have to work at it extra hard. And that will make the difference in your son's life. We have already seen that *involvement* in kids' lives is what makes great kids. And since you aren't a man who can model fatherhood, you must learn the traits of the Author of Fatherhood and point your boys to Him. And you can surround yourself with good assistant coaches.

The Coaching Staff

Because I try to live my life with the Author of Fatherhood as the man in my boys' lives and the head of our home, I try to remember to bring every decision that needs to be made for the boys to Him. Sometimes I forget, and my worrying gets the best of me. Luckily, God is always right there to remind me that He is still involved.

When we moved, I was so incredibly stressed about my seventh grader having to switch schools that I stayed up nights worrying. How would he cope in this much bigger, secular school when he was raised in a small Christian school? The day we went to the office to sign him up for classes, this very cute eighth-grade girl struck up a conversation. She was so confident, telling us all about her family and that she had switched schools recently and loved it here, and that she would look out for my son since they had the same lunch break. My mind was a little at ease. Then, in the course of our conversation, she mentioned her uncle, and I recognized the name. I had known her uncle years ago because he was the brother of a girl I had helped when she was in high school and had a crisis pregnancy—about 13 years ago. This was that baby!

> God uses people in our lives to be the hands-on touch our hearts need.

It brings tears to my eyes even now thinking that only God could have orchestrated that encounter. God was re-assuring me that He really did have everything under control, and He really was looking out for my son. I had no cause for concern—He was on the job!

I love it when He gives us those little reassurances that we are not parenting alone. But we do have to be alert to recognize them, and we do have to continue to bring our needs before Him. By bringing even the small decisions to Him, I also am able to give Him the credit when things go right.

God uses people in our lives to be the hands-on touch our hearts need. It's important to remember that everyone in our boys' lives is going to have an impact on them—some positive and some negative. While you can be your son's primary coach, you are going to have to rely on a large coaching staff to help you—your church family, your family, friends, professionals, even coaches. I pray more earnestly for these relationships. And while I am speaking figuratively about coaches in our lives, the boys will have real coaches in their lives as well. Soccer coaches, football coaches, baseball coaches. Sometimes in these sports the other boys have a father coaching them, and they are to be valued and applauded for the great fathers they are! I certainly hope my own boys are able to coach their sons—or daughters—someday. Point it out to your sons as something to look forward to—not as just another thing they don't have.

Seeing other good men in action can help our sons learn about being slow to anger or how to lose or win graciously. Unfortunately, some men will be models of what you do *not* want your boys to be. Point that out too. Giving them the opportunity to see both good and bad behavior modeled is important. Just as people have misconceptions about you and your parenting ability as a mom raising a son, your sons are going to have misconceptions about what it means to be a man. Give them the opportunity to witness real strength in action with coaches, relatives, and friends. God can use all of them, and it doesn't have to be something you set up or artificially create. Just get *involved*.

My sons have been very lucky to have the coaches

they have had. I was especially concerned about football. Now there's a sport where the parents get a little out of control—moms and dads! But in every case I have volunteered to be the team mom, got involved, got to know the coaches, and have observed what they were modeling for my sons. And they have been awesome! The high school coach in our area actually is involved in men's Bible study and invites the boys to his home. My younger son's soccer coach and his wife are so incredibly good with the boys— encouraging, never putting down any of the kids if their skills aren't the best. Always teaching them more. And I'll tell you that this coach led his team to an undefeated championship while doing it! God can bring men into their lives to model good character.

Training Makes You Tired

There are going to be days when you feel like you are sinking yourself. It's not easy to do the job of two people. It's a matter of sheer numbers. It's twice the workload if you are raising boys alone. More than twice if you factor in the learning you must do for helping them become men after God's own heart. It's OK to just say no to the busyness of life when it does not directly impact you raising your boys.

I have two wonderful pastors at church, Chico and Carlos. There are many things I could be doing to serve in

> **Sometimes we have to measure what we are doing against what it is we are trying to accomplish—and that is raising strong men of God.**

ministry at the church, but they guard my time for me. Sometimes they ask my advice on something, but they don't ask me to take on another task. It's not because they don't think I'm capable, but they are mature enough in their own ministry lives to know to not overburden me in my life. Sometimes when I get riled about a new project and want to jump in with both feet, Chico will ask me, "Which part of the world are you going to take over now? Don't you think you ought to finish the corner you've got?" He's always right, of course. Sometimes we have to measure what we are doing against what it is we are trying to accomplish—and that is raising strong men of God.

Don't let a social life get in the way of raising your sons. Weigh what takes up your time against the time you actually have available. Work? You have to do that. Laundry? You have to do that—and it never ends with two boys! Paying bills? You have to do that. Wasting the day watching TV? You don't have to do that, but once in a while it just feels good. But just once in a while.

No Creative Worrying

There are going to be enough days with real worries

without you causing them. I even have a little plaque on my desk that says, "I have faced many of life's trials, many of them never even happened." I'm afraid worry is one of my terrible weaknesses. I worry. A friend of mine told me once that I am so good at worrying that I could be considered a *creative worrier*. I can worry about things that *might* happen in every kind of scenario you can possibly imagine. I like to think I'm making contingency plans just in case something terrible happens. In planning for earthquakes, it's good to stock supplies and be prepared for the worst. But in raising boys, it might not be the best idea to start down the path of worrying about things that will very likely never happen.

When I became a single mom with a newborn and a four-year-old, I had many legitimate fears and worries. *How was I going to pay bills? How was I going to get any sleep?* I had a newborn with no one to help spell me in the night, and I was working full time. How would I raise boys who are foreign creatures to me? What would happen to the boys without a father in the home? These were real worries. But do you know that my biggest concern was that my boys would never learn to stand up when they used the bathroom? Yes. This was my greatest fear.

I envisioned my boys growing up to be sissy men because they had no father to teach them to wrestle, fight, burp, or watch football games on Sunday afternoon. In my head, I just knew that when they were in junior high they would be picked on by the more macho boys who had dads, they would get beat up by the sports jocks, and I would have failed them! Yes. This was my real concern with my newborn and my four-year-old.

I realize that some of you other mothers might be thinking that this was a pretty stupid thing to fear. I mean, usually our fears over the bathroom are about the first time we are out in public and our boys are too old to go in the women's restroom with us. But to me it was very real. As you can see, I spent a great deal of time thinking about it. I even had a plan. Yes, my older son could teach my younger son.

So when my Nathan was old enough to start potty training, I was sure that he learned exactly how he was to do it—standing up. I even found a "Potty Book" that showed a little boy standing up to go potty so he would know that's how men did it.

A couple years later I was going to graduate school nights to go back and get that degree that was interrupted years ago. I commuted to Biola University in Los Angeles two and three nights a week. That's a two hour drive each way, plus four hours of class time—then homework. My boys were three and seven when I started grad school, and they spent many nights with my mom, my sister's family, and my very good friends, Bunmi and Tolu.

Bunmi and Tolu have the perfect family. They have been married forever, are financially well off, own a large home, and have three kids. Bunmi is a stay-at-home mom. They are what everyone would consider a perfect family. Tolu was wonderful with my boys. It was such a blessing to have my boys spending many nights with my brother-in-law, my father, and in Tolu's home to see real men in everyday situations. The Lord used those men and that time in our lives.

One day I was hanging out at Bunmi's house. She was cleaning, and I was having coffee and visiting. She went into the bathroom to pick up clothes off the floor and casually mentioned, "Now why would this seat be up? You know I do not let any men in our home stand up to go to the bathroom. Did the boys tell you? I make everyone sit down because I just can't have that mess in my home. Tolu has gotten used to it. Have the boys ever mentioned that?" I just about spit my coffee out. This perfect family had been teaching my boys to SIT!

I laughed out loud. I had spent years worrying that my boys would not be manly enough because they had no father in the home to teach them, and Tolu's manhood wasn't threatened to go to the bathroom sitting down!

This perfect family was training their boys to sit! What a good chuckle God must get when we scurry around worrying about the most trivial things. Maybe God was trying to show me just how silly I was and reassure me that my worries about their training and my training abilities were unfounded.

Coffee with a Friend

Things to Remember:

- *To train up a child* requires action.

- You can raise a champion husband and father

- Your son is your work project—get every little tool you can.

- You are training with God in the picture.

- Anyone, then, who knows the good he ought to do and doesn't do it, sins (James 4:17).
- He has showed you, O man, what is good. And what does the LORD require of you? To act justly and to love mercy and to walk humbly with your God (Micah 6:8).

4 Separation & Situations
There's No Substitute for Time

BECAUSE OF THEIR FEELINGS OF ABANDONMENT, my boys were very insecure in the years following the break up. Every day when I dropped them off at school, my oldest—about five at the time—asked me over and over if I was *really* going to pick him up after school. He was afraid I would forget. If I was even a few minutes late, he was deeply worried that I wouldn't return.

My job required me to travel occasionally. The baby was not a problem, but my older son was afraid I was never coming back. That is when I started bringing them Beanie Babies every time I traveled. I told them that I had to come back because I had to give them the Beanies. This seemed to set their minds at ease. I also started wearing two silver rings whenever I traveled. When I talked on the phone with them while I was gone, they would ask, "Are you wearing your rings so you don't forget?" The rings were to remind me to pray for them and to come home—one ring for each boy. The rings were something tangible they understood, not just words or promises they had no concept of. Too many promises had already been broken in their lives.

When You Can't Help It

I tried to keep my traveling to a minimum. If the trip wasn't absolutely necessary, I didn't go. I struggle with the guilt of being a single parent, always feeling if I had made better choices my children wouldn't have to suffer the pain of going without. I make them a priority, going to every ball game and staying involved in their lives. I measure everything against my personal mission statement, which is to raise two godly men. Everything else takes second place.

One day I got a call from the Capitol in Sacramento. I had been named Woman of the Year, and they were calling to make travel arrangements for me to come up and spend the day and receive the award. Wow! That is very exciting! I was getting the award because of my work with women in crisis and in our community. The day I was to receive the award was the same day as my son's first baseball game. When I realized that, I told the lady who had called me that I would be honored to fly up and receive the Women of the Year Award, but I couldn't stay for the dinner and festivities because I needed to get back by 5 o'clock for my son's 6 o'clock game. I think she dropped the phone.

She explained to me that this award was quite an honor and that the senator would be spending his day with me and that I absolutely must stay with such an important person for such an important event. I explained to her that an important person, my son, was expecting me at home that night, and I could not and would not let him down. She

reluctantly made the travel arrangements as I had request-
ed, and I was so excited that I would be getting the award
and showing my son how important he is to me.

I flew up on the appointed day and received my
award. There was a big ceremony, lots of pictures with important people were taken, and I got back to the airport in
plenty of time to catch my plane back to see my son's
game. Perfect. But the plane broke down, and I didn't get
home until after 9 P.M.

I was riddled with anxiety. I had moved heaven and
earth so I wouldn't let my son down, turned down a big
dinner with a senator to be held in my
honor so I could be woman of the year
in my son's eyes. Circumstances beyond
my control caused me to fail my son. I
remembered him sitting on the front
porch waiting for his dad who never
showed up. It hurt me beyond words.

**The fact is,
nothing I do can
make up for my
son's loss of time
with his father.**

Of course, this was different. I called my son from the
airport and explained what had happened. He was happy
as a clam because he was staying with his best buddy on the
team anyway. My guilt, however, was overwhelming. I was
still carrying the baggage from my failed marriage, and I
was trying to make it up to my son. The fact is, nothing I
do can make up for my son's loss of time with his father. It

is beyond my control—just as that's plane engine trouble was beyond my control.

All I can do is say what I mean and mean what I say. That was one of my graduate school professor's favorite lines. Another one is "walk the talk." That is a trait God the Father lives for us every day, and something we can model for our sons whether we are male or female. As mothers, we can keep our word and give time to our sons, modeling God the Father for them. We can never compensate for what their earthly fathers may or may not have done. But we can give our sons glimpses of the original Father.

All that being said, I was still hopping mad at the airlines at the time, and I wrote a not-so-kind letter telling them so. My son had been hurt, and I let them know about it. They sent two roundtrip tickets along with their sincere apologies so that I could take him to the Capitol. So my son and I traveled to Sacramento, and a dear friend in the senate gave us a tour that included the house floor and secret places in the Capitol Building. My son had a great time! It was way better than an award dinner, and it showed my son that my intentions were to never leave him or forsake him. Just like God the Father tells all of us in Deut. 31:8: "The LORD himself goes before you and will be with you; he will never leave you nor forsake you. Do not be afraid; do not be discouraged."

Now when I tell my son something has come up and I really can't make it somewhere, he knows it must be important and it's OK—I'm coming back. It didn't necessarily have to be something as dramatic as turning down dinner at the Capitol for the Woman of the Year award, but it was worth it to show my son he could trust that he is my top priority.

Because I Said So

Sometimes you just have to back up your words with your actions. When your walk matches your talk, that is character. And character is what you want your boys to learn. Sometimes you only need to remember to do the talking.

My younger son, Nathan, and I play with words. Ever since he was old enough to talk, when I tucked him in at night we went back and forth, "I love you to the moon."

"I love you to the moon and back."

"I love you to the moon and back and to Pluto."

"I love you to the moon and back and to Pluto and then Saturn."

"I love you to the moon and back and to Pluto and then Saturn and then back to the moon"

This ritual lasted for several minutes, until he gave up and said, "OK, you love me!"

Now when I say, "Nathan, I love you." He simply says, "I know." And I say, "How do you know?" and he says, "Because you tell me so."

When I was growing up, "because I said so" were words I promised myself I would not say to my own kids! They meant something different when spoken as a last resort in a command. Now "because I said so" says they can trust that I will always love them and be here for them. If I say so, it must be true. My words are consistent, and they consistently match my actions.

When I pressed Nathan the other day about the words *just because I said so*, he said, "Mom, come on. You take care of us, feed us, buy us the things we need. Of course you love us—that's how I know." He's right. I pointed out that's how he knows God loves him too. Because He says so in the Bible and because He backs up those words with actions by taking care of us, listening to our prayers, providing for us. All the things He says He will do, He can be trusted to do.

The Sunrise

How did you like the sunrise this morning? Do you know that if the world were to spin just a fraction off course we would spin right out of control—right out of orbit? Our weather would destroy us, tides would shift and flood us; it would be chaos. But God stayed up all night keeping the world spinning just perfectly so you would wake up this morning just like you did yesterday and just like you will tomorrow and just like the next day. God said He would look after you, and He is keeping His word.

Every morning there is an opportunity to teach your sons about commitment and consistency.

And why do you worry about clothes? See how the lilies of the field grow. They do not labor or spin. Yet I tell you that not even Solomon in all his splendor was dressed like one of these (Matt. 6:28-29).

Every morning there is an opportunity to teach your sons about commitment and consistency. Did you wake up this morning and the world was spinning out of control? No. And I can guarantee that you will not wake up to chaos tomorrow, because God is a God of order. Point that out to your kids every morning. God makes the sunrise just for them—every day. Take the time to train them, to teach them, and to coach them that God is a man to be counted on. Boys need consistency. They need to know they can rely on us and on God. And that takes time.

The only way to do that for them, to instill that in them, is to model consistency until they live it and respect it in their own lives.

Praying for Firemen

In our family, when we are driving in the car and we hear a siren, we take a moment and say a prayer for the victims of whatever has happened and for the firemen who are on their way to help. We take turns doing the praying, and I pray with my eyes open, obviously. But we always, every time, say a prayer.

One morning we were rushing to get to school because I was running late, as usual. Nate was in his first week of kindergarten, and I was concerned about him being on the playground in the mornings with the big kids, so I usually drove the boys to school and then stayed for a little while to keep an eye on him. Of course, I stayed back far enough that they could walk in all by themselves. They needed their independence, you know, by kindergarten and fourth grade.

I got to the playground with coffee in hand, and there were more moms there than usual. "Can you believe what happened?" I had no idea what they were talking about. "I can't believe those towers came down—they say 50 thousand people a day go through there!" It was 7:30 A.M. on the West Coast—September 11, 2001. I had not seen the news that morning because we were rushing around to get out the door. I was in shock initially and refused to believe it.

Friends had just come back from New York and had stood on the observation deck of the Twin Towers. I couldn't believe what the moms were telling me. Then they said something that pierced my heart, "It's been on the news all morning—every channel. Didn't you see it?"

They had practiced time and again their disaster drill, and when it was really needed, they knew exactly what to do.

CJ had been watching TV all morning as I was rushing to get Nate ready. What had they seen that I had missed? I found the boys on the playground and went to them calm as could be and said I needed to tell them something terrible, and I wanted to talk to them about it before all the kids at school started talking about it. As it turned out, both boys had already seen the images that morning. CJ said there were no cartoons, so he had watched the footage of the towers coming down over and over and the people running and scared. I asked him what he thought, and he said, "I prayed for the firemen going to work in it and the victims they were going to help." And that was it. They had practiced time and again their disaster drill, and when it was really needed, they knew exactly what to do.

Of course, the boys rallied over the next few months just as the rest of the country did. They drew pictures and wrote a letter of encouragement to the president. And we dealt with the anger and frustration because of the human suffering. They were little men right from the beginning—ready to defend us all. But it was the commitment in their lives to turn to God when they heard a siren that prepared them to do the same when it was needed on a much grander scale. We should not forget that grand scale. Helping our boys pray about each siren every day will give them a rock they can lean on when things go terribly wrong. A habit in their lives.

God Uses People

When I was growing up, my mom was raising three kids alone most of the time while my dad was deployed. She made it a habit to build God into our lives. There were many times I hated having to go to church—especially when I was in junior high. We were involved in a youth program every Wednesday night. I earned an award for memorizing more than 300 verses. I wasn't thrilled about it at the time, and I couldn't quote them all for you chapter and verse right now, but when things go terribly wrong in my life, I am somehow able to recall those verses when I need them. I may not be able to give you the reference, but I know the essence of the verses. They became habit in my life—something to lean on when I need them.

Getting us involved in a strong church family was one

of the greatest things my mom did. Those friends who surrounded her and helped her mend fences and fix the plumbing and took her son to the church softball games are the same friends my parents have today. The same friends our whole family has today nearly 40 years later. I know I could call on "Aunt" Donna and "Uncle" Bob Rowan any day of the week for anything, and they would come running. The Joyces, the Rowans, the Briggs, Pastor Forge—they were all there for my mom when my dad was away, and they are still here for us today. God uses His people in the church to work like a body, everyone doing his or her part to fulfill God's promise to be the husband to the widow and father to the fatherless.

Now the body is not made up of one part but of many. If the foot should say, "Because I am not a hand, I do not belong to the body, it would not for that reason cease to be part of the body (1 Cor. 12:14-15).

The eye cannot say to the hand, "I don't need you!" And the head cannot say to the feet, "I don't need you!" On the contrary, those parts of the body that seem to be weaker are indispensable, and the parts that we think are less honorable we treat with special honor. And the parts that are unpresentable are treated with special modesty, while our presentable parts need no special treatment. But God has combined the members of the body and has given greater honor to the parts that lacked it, so that there should be no division in the body, but that its parts should have equal concern for each other. If one part suffers, every part suffers with it; if one part is honored, every part rejoices with it. Now you are the body of Christ, and each one of you is a part of it" (1 Cor. 12:21-27).

You Are Not Alone

You don't have to raise your sons alone. In fact, you are *not* doing it alone. I was getting my oil changed the other day and noticed that the oil change place got smart and put in a nail salon for the ladies who are waiting on their cars. I guess they finally realized that women are sometimes the ones taking care of the cars these days with so many of us heads of the household. So I got a manicure and pedicure —a special treat for me—and I especially loved that I was multitasking and saving time. And the young woman working there and I got to talking about moms raising boys.

We both laughed and cried sharing stories about her friends who are single moms. We talked about adopted kids and other unique family situations, and when I said to her, "I wish all moms raising sons could know they are not doing this alone," she said, "That's because they are not."

Now I knew what I meant when I said it, but I had to ask her what she meant. She said, "I was just talking to a single mom with a boy in my child's class and now that I know her unique needs, I can go home and pray for her. Now I have just told you about her, and you can pray for her. And you will write in your book about the needs of single moms and everyone who reads it will pray for all the single moms in the world and their needs. And God hears all our requests. And even if the woman in my child's class never knows you or about your book and all the people reading it, the Lord knows and hears our prayers, and He will watch out for her that many times more!"

> We don't need to know each and every need of every mom raising boys out there. God knows them all and hears our prayers.

I hadn't thought of it that way. We don't need to know each and every need of every mom raising boys out there. God knows them all and hears our prayers. I felt *really* good about the use of my time. Not only did I get my oil changed and my nails done, but we had a mini Bible study and support group too.

Miracle of Time

The reality is, if we weren't multitasking, we could never keep up with our boys. It is only with God's intervention that we are able to accomplish what we do in a day. People ask me "Where do you find the time to do all that?" When I count the minutes and hours in a day and look at all that must be done, it simply isn't physically possible. I am unable to explain how it all gets done. You know what I'm talking about. There are those times when the laundry seems endless, and your son gets grass stains on his uniform the day before the big tournament because he just "felt" like playing in the park with his uniform on for some unexplainable reason, and the dog throws up on the carpet, and you forgot to lay something out for dinner. Somehow, the following week, Saturday rolls around and all those things got taken care of, and you have moved on to a whole new list of urgent matters that require your attention. How can you explain it without calling it a miracle?

Point these miracles out to your son. Tell him that you can't explain how it all works out, but you and he can both trust that God is still present in your home, making sure it all gets done. If you take the time to point that out to him now, it will be his own habit to rely on when he is a father in his own home someday and he is called upon to be the reflection of the miracle worker as he helps his wife get it all done. He will know he can rely on the Lord to be present every step of the way.

Time is tricky. It's a limited commodity—especially for

It is important that we consistently walk the talk so that we can point our boys to the Author of Fatherhood.

single moms who are trying to do the work of two people. You won't be able to have four-hour talks with your son in the middle of the day. You will have to steal special moments a few at a time and be present when you can and pray that God will give you opportunities in those moments to live and model His character. That's just a fact of your life.

It is important that we consistently walk the talk so that we can point our boys to the Author of Fatherhood. He makes the sun rise each and every day, because He gave His word. And He would cause the sun to rise each morning even if your son were the only person on the planet, not just because He has to for others—but just for your son. Take the time to teach him that.

Coffee with a Friend

Things to Remember:

- Find tangible ways to reassure your sons and direct them to the Lord—He will never leave them or you!

- Time is the most important thing you can give—to your kids and to God.

- Make sure your sons spend time with good male role models.

5 Fathers & Futures
How Do You Pass On Macho?

LET'S FACE IT, BOYS FIGHT. They wrestle, and they get in the dirt. Frankly, I love that about them. They are training to be the protectors God intended them to be. Let them. But give them guidance along the way. My boys have been taught to stand up for the little guy and to never bully others.

When CJ was in kindergarten, he was one of the "cool" kids, if that's possible for kindergarteners. These kids ran the school even at a young age—mostly because their moms were involved in the leadership of the school. One little boy in the class was a little slower than the others, and CJ's best friend picked on this particular little boy a lot. When CJ was planning his birthday party, I insisted he invite the little boy that was the "outcast," and we made special arrangements because this little boy had never been to a birthday party before and his learning disabilities caused him to be a bit fearful of the new experience.

I knew I didn't want to model that attitude for my son.

When I told CJ the plan, he said he didn't want to invite him because his best friend didn't have to invite this little boy to his party. CJ said his best friend's mom told the boys it was because the slower boy was too much trouble and a little weird. Well, I knew I wasn't going to get any support from that family. But I also knew that I didn't want to model that attitude for my son.

CJ's best friend lived in a two-parent home, very well off, with a father in the home to give guidance. The family represented all that the world calls *stable*. I saw it as an example of the fact that having a man in the home doesn't automatically mean that God's character is being modeled. I needed to teach my son about being a man *in spite* of the message coming from this traditional home. This was also an opportunity to point out to my young son that people made fun of this boy with learning disabilities and excluded him simply because he was different. I asked my son how he would feel if people did that to him because he was from a single-parent home. Would Jesus do that to him or to this boy if He were here? I had this conversation with my son and his best friend one day.

We were in the car coming home from school, and I asked the boys how they thought Jesus would treat the child in their class. At first, CJ's friend was giving me the same answers he had heard from his parents—the boy is annoying, I can't have fun when he is around, it's too much trouble to have him come to our party. I said to CJ's best friend, "What if someone came up to CJ and said he was stupid because he didn't have a dad?" His little friend said without hesitation, "I would beat him up! I wouldn't even need any help. If someone said that to CJ, I would just beat him up, and I could!"

I had no doubt that he could. There was never any question of that. I explained that is how Jesus feels about this little boy—about all little boys. They are like His best friends, and when someone is mean to them, He wants to protect them from being hurt like that. Both boys understood, and the little boy came to our party and had a great time.

The family ended up leaving the school after that year for a different school where the child could learn at his own pace, and he is doing great today. Before they left, his mom stopped me in the hall at school. With tears in her eyes, she said, "I know what you did for my son," and she choked a bit. "I just want to thank you. I never told the principal the problems my son was going through with the boys picking on him, because I didn't want to make it worse than it already was. But I prayed about it. Thank you is all I can say as a mother who was hurt for her son." I cried myself after she walked away. I know how defensive and protective I get for my boys with all they have to deal with; I can't even imagine the hurt she experienced when her child with disabilities had to learn to deal with bullies in kindergarten. I was thankful that God led us to answer her prayers for her son while I taught my own son the importance of looking out for others.

> **I was thankful that God led us to answer her prayers for her son while I taught my own son the importance of looking out for others.**

Fights in Life

As it turns out, CJ has grown into quite a big man. He plays center on his football team and inherited his father's muscular body. I'm glad he learned humility early to go along with his masculine physique. Humility has allowed CJ to be a stronger man in every sense of the word.

I wanted my sons to be able to defend themselves, and they know Karate, play football, and lift weights. I encouraged this not just because they might need to defend themselves or others, but because their pediatrician has always pounded it into my head every time we see her. "They should always be in at least two sports" she says. "Boys are too active, and if they aren't kept busy, they'll just cause trouble." Our doctor may be a little old-school, but she is right about that. Boys are active, and if for no other reason than I know at our next appointment I am going to have to rattle off at least two sports they are active in, I keep them busy.

Now that they are bigger, we have three rules in our house about fighting.

1. Always stand up for the little guy.
2. Never start a fight. (Don't fight if you don't have to.)
3. If it is started, you finish it.

My boys know that whatever the politically correct thing of the day is on violence, they would be in more trouble once they got home if they stood by and let a little guy or disabled child get picked on or beat up. Every boy is different and every boy will have his own skill set to use to stick up for the little guys in life. Sometimes it is being a man of character in the workplace. It might be speaking out against what is "popular" to say or believe. It's not necessarily going to be a physical confrontation, but there will always be a fight to be fought. Men of character take a stand for what is right in whatever way God directs them.

> Men of character take a stand for what is right in whatever way God directs them.

"A man's mind plans his way, but the Lord directs his path" (Prov. 16:9).

God the Father never backed down from sticking up for the underdog. When Jesus was here on earth, He met the woman at the well, a sinner and cheater shunned by society. He stood up in the crowd and stopped it from stoning the woman outside the city walls, placing himself between her and those that would hurt her. He challenged, "Let those without sin throw the first stone." Jesus also protected the children when the disciples wanted to push them away. He told the children to come to Him. He died on the cross for us—a horrible, painful death. He stuck up for us even to the point of death. That is macho and what I want my boys to model themselves after, even when it is not so convenient to have the slower boy at the party because he's a little more work and might dampen the fun.

How Much More Does He Love You?

It's not just important that my boys understand that real men look out for others. They need to know that God looks out for others, and He will always look out for them. It's very hard to explain to our kids that God loves them more than we do. It's even hard for me to grasp sometimes. The Author of Fatherhood has crafted fathers to be defenders. Each man will do that in different ways.

My two boys are very different. My oldest is the athletic type; he runs and lifts weights just for the fun of it. It's hard for me to relate to that because I am not athletic in the least. He is also a thinker, and he cares deeply about the injustices in the world and wants to make things right.

My younger son is outgoing and friendly and extremely creative. He is friends with everyone at a new school—including the adults—before the first day is over. He stays busy with painting or drawing or writing. He always has some new artistic endeavor in process. He is drawn to sports that are more individual. (He has to meet his two-sport quota for the pediatrician too.) My older son is more drawn to team sports.

Although they are very different, they are also similar in their qualities of character and discipline. They just express those qualities in different ways. It's not personality types and experiences that determine their "manliness." I worried so much about the lack of a male influence in our home, and then they turned out to be men anyway. God the Father made sure of that.

Keeping Up

Granted, I can't go play tackle football with them like some dads might. But I do get out there and play with them. I get involved in all their sports. I had to adapt a bit to their more rough and tumble ways, but before I knew it, we were adapted to each other.

When Nathan was in first grade, we had a horrible experience with a teacher. She was new, and she had never taught first graders. Although she had children of her own, I learned they were all girls. She seemed to think all kids would behave as her girls behaved, so having those four boys in her class that first year could be described as "shock and awe."

Let's just say that boys are active. They hardly ever sit

still to color. Nor do they enjoy reading about kittens or playing house. They like to run and jump and play kick ball and soccer. They love to have mud fights and throw rocks. This poor teacher and the four boys in her class spent most of that year in the principal's office. I can't say for sure it was because of the boys, but she didn't return to teach the next year.

You and I do not have the option of going into another line of work. We don't get to just quit when the boys decide to jump off the roof today. We have to try to catch them when they jump, and prevent them from doing it again.

Recruit a Friend

Even if you are already doing a great job of raising boys, sooner or later questions and issues regarding sex are going to enter your world. You may need a little back up when that day arrives.

My friend Ann, the single mom with the nine kids, has several teenage and adult sons now. Even though she raised them to respect women and she had many talks with them about sex and how to conduct themselves, one of her middle teenage sons stumbled into trouble when curiosity got the best of him. One of Ann's close friends lives near the boys' school, and the kids go to her house after school to hang out and share rides. This family has always been a pillar for Ann and her family to lean on, and a great source of support. This made it doubly difficult when the friend had to tell Ann that her son had been making phone-sex calls from her phone and running up a huge phone bill. He had also rented some pornography on their TV from the cable service.

There are times we'll need to reach out to others— a brother, grandparent, pastor, or friend.

Through some research by all the adults, they confirmed that it was Ann's son. When asked, he freely admitted it. Ann paid her friends' bills and demanded that her son earn the money to reimburse her. The hardest part for Ann was determining a way to connect with her son and understand where this curiosity came from.

She contacted a good friend at church who had been a coach and youth leader to her boys for years. The friend gladly accepted the challenge to meet with Ann's son and help work through the situation. Ann was fortunate to be able to reach out to this man—someone in God's family—to guide her son and help him see the Author of Fatherhood.

We will be able to handle most situations ourselves, but there are times we'll need to reach out to others—a brother, grandparent, pastor, or friend. The important thing is to reach out and call on the Body of Christ to help us when we need it.

You Are a Mother of Boys When . . .

I realized just what a boys' mom I was when I babysat for a friend's two little girls. How hard could it be? I'd heard that girls were easy. They were quiet, and they like to color and play with Barbie dolls. I figured the four kids would entertain each other. I had always thought I'd like to have a daughter, so it sounded like great fun. I was miserable. The girls squealed, tattled, and took exception when the boys used their Barbie dolls to fight with G.I. Joe's guns. Those of you with boys *and* girls know what I am talking about. After all the years I longed for a little girl, I realized that I am not a mom for girls; I am a mom for boys! I had been mothering boys for so long that the high-pitched squealing and giggling at *everything* was more than I could take! My boys could be wrestling to the death, rolling around on the floor, and I wouldn't so much as flinch or interrupt a conversation on the phone. But the day I spent babysitting those two girls was one of the longest days of my life. Yes, boys are different. And I love it!

Macho Man Too Soon

When you're a single parent, you get so much advice that you're sure you will never fall into any of the common traps. You hear "don't date through your kids," "don't treat your kids as if they're adults," "don't feel guilty and over-indulge your kids to compensate for the divorce." Then I noticed a friend letting her son dictate the schedule for the entire family. Who was the adult here?

You might think your son can be the man of the house. But that role is God's, even if there is a male adult in your home.

Coffee with a Friend

Things to Remember:

- How do you help them be "macho" men? Encourage their differences. Help them excel in things that may not be in your comfort zone.

- Repetition equals habit. They say it takes seven times for a media message to take hold. Repeat, repeat in a different way, and repeat again.

- Kids will go to what feels familiar. They need consistency. So build the Heavenly Father into their lives consistently. It's never too late to start.

6 Character & Commitment
There's No Such Thing as a Perfect Mom—or Son

Do not be misled: "Bad company corrupts good character"
(1 Cor. 15:33)."

BAD THINGS HAPPEN TO GOOD PEOPLE. It's not just a cliché; it's true. I find in talking to single moms and women who used to be single moms who are now married and raising kids, that they tend to beat themselves up for their past mistakes and their relationships with their sons. It's important to understand that everyone runs across problems—two parent homes, single-parent homes, grand-parent homes. There is no escaping the inevitable. How we respond and handle those problems is what makes the difference. And with God the Father stepping in to help, you can handle anything.

> Consider it pure joy, my brothers, whenever you face trials of many kinds, because you know that the testing of your faith develops perseverance. Perseverance must finish its work so that you may be mature and complete, not lacking anything" (James 1:2-4).

> Not only so, but we also rejoice in our sufferings, because we know that suffering produces perseverance; perseverance, character; and character, hope. And hope does not disappoint us, because God has poured out his love into our hearts by the Holy Spirit, whom he has given us (Rom. 5:3).

> For this very reason, make every effort to add to your faith goodness; and to goodness, knowledge;

and to knowledge, self-control; and to self-control, perseverance; and to perseverance, godliness; and to godliness, brotherly kindness; and to brotherly kindness, love (2 Peter 1:5-7).

Several years ago, a short story was written about me and my work with women in crisis. I went to a pregnancy center to meet with the director, and one of the volunteers came up to me and said, "Oh! I just read about you. When I read that, I thought *I want to be her!*" I just laughed and said, "Yeah, when I read it, I thought *I want to be her too!*"

There is no such thing as the perfect mom.

It's easy to look at other people and think they are doing better than you. In a short, 500-word essay about a specific topic, the author doesn't mention the laundry that's piling up, her impatience with her kids, or the bills that aren't getting paid. When we are having one of those days when everything goes wrong, it's easy to get down on ourselves and think everyone else is doing it better. But that just isn't true. Don't buy into the lie that you aren't able to do it as well as the next person. You're doing great! There is no such thing as the perfect mom. The grass always seems greener in the yard next door, but the fact is, my house is a mess most of the time and chaos is my middle name. The things I am really good at, you might not be great at. And the things I lack in, I'm sure you have in spades! You may not have written a book—but I bet your house is cleaner or you can play an instrument or carry a tune or cook. I can't do those things. Concentrate on the great things you are doing and can do, and try to never compare yourself to others.

Desert People

One day I heard my son in his room. He was obviously upset but mostly angry. I asked him what was wrong, and as usual I got "Nothin'." So I kept on him because he was clearly angry about *something*. Turns out one of his friends at school got a dirt bike for his birthday, and my son lashed out at me, "If you had made better choices and we had a dad in the house, I could have a dirt bike and we could go to the desert every weekend."

That was a loaded statement; I could have taken it in several different directions. But before I launched into why a dad wasn't in the home or what not having a dad meant to him, I decided to take a deep breath and explore what he was really saying before I jumped head first into what I *heard* him say. After a few moments of listening to him, I realized that this was not one of those "I-want-a-dad" moments. It was actually an "I-want-a-dirt-bike" moment.

I started out by explaining that having a dad in the

home had nothing to do with getting a dirt bike. Even if we had a dad in our home, that wouldn't make us desert people. I refuse to camp, and I hate the desert! In fact, guys who are outdoorsy are automatically screened out of my life, so the chances of him *ever* having a dad who likes camping and living in the desert are slim to none. If we had a dad in the house, he would most likely be interested in the same things we are —horses, surfing, and we would spend weekends at football and soccer games and summers visiting relatives and winters getting away to the mountains to snowboard. We probably wouldn't have a dad in the house who left us doing those things while he went out to the desert. But several of the families we were friends with were desert people and had asked CJ to go with them several times. If he wanted to join them for a couple weekends, he was more than welcome to do that. And that resolved that issue.

> Sometimes, when we moms are tempted to jump on the guilt bandwagon and begin beating ourselves up because there is no dad in the house, it's really just about our son wanting a dirt bike.

Sometimes, when we moms are tempted to jump on the guilt bandwagon and begin beating ourselves up because there is no dad in the house, it's really just about our son wanting a dirt bike. Too often, we go right out and buy that dirt bike for any number of reasons—most of which boil down to guilt. Maybe we feel guilty because they have been through so much in their lives and we don't want them to be disappointed any more. Or maybe we feel that our sons shouldn't have to suffer as a result of our bad choices. Or maybe we don't want them to feel left out because other kids who live in two-income households have everything they want.

Whatever the reasons, giving them more toys isn't going to solve those issues, and it won't help shape their character.

Other People's Homes

We never know what really goes on in other people's homes. Be careful not to fall into the trap of thinking that it must be better than what goes on in yours. It's not healthy for us to think that way or for our sons to get in the habit of thinking that if only we had more money we'd be happy. If only I was prettier, I would be happy. If only I was thinner, I would be happy. If only I had a dad, I would be happy. We know these things are not true, so why do we allow our sons to believe them?

My oldest son learned the hard way. For years he had not heard from his father. Then, out of the blue, his father got an attorney to help him lower his child support, and although he lived in another state, to get his child support lowered he had to see the kids. So the court ordered that the boys spend one week with their father in the winter when they were five and nine years old. My nine-year-old had built his father up so much in his mind that I was afraid of what was going to happen. Letting him go spend a week with a man he hadn't seen in years—or even talked to on the phone—made me a nervous wreck. But it was so important to my son because he believed his father was perfect and that if his father was in his life it would fill the lonely place.

I made it a big deal—bought them all new clothes and packed travel games for the trip. I tried to make it a grand adventure. That was for the boys, and also it was to help me get through handing these precious boys over to a man they had no relationship with and I did not trust. The big day came and went and the boys were gone for a week with their dad.

When they came home from the trip, CJ was a different child. He had aged years during that week. The first thing he said was, "Mom, they are not like us." We talked about it a long time. What CJ had learned about a father were the characteristics of God the Father, and this man he visited was not like that at all. He wasn't the perfect husband and father CJ had imagined him to be. CJ spent his week looking out for Nathan and eager to come home.

> There is no perfect family, no perfect home, no perfect father—other than God the Father.

It was hard for me to hear about their week. "I wouldn't want to live there, Mom." Even though I had my own issues with their father and knew that no one is perfect, I still would have liked for him to have been that perfect dad for my boys' sake—if only for a week. But the lesson the boys learned was invaluable. Absence does make the heart grow fonder. CJ's father had become larger than life in CJ's eyes. When CJ saw him in real life, he realized that just having a man in the home would not make everything right. Living with reality for a week helped CJ realize that there is no perfect family, no perfect home, no perfect father—other than God the Father.

Perfect Does Not Equal Character

Once I was in the middle of a heated conflict at the office. People had chosen sides and there was a lot of back-biting and game-playing going on to try and get the upper hand. In frustration, I said to a friend, "Why doesn't he just be a man and handle the situation face-to-face?"

My coworker replied, "Dana, you are more a man than most men I know!

It wasn't a statement about my gender. It was a statement about my character. Certain character traits are attributed to "being a man." Being perfect is certainly not a requirement, but standing up for what is right is a trait we attribute to being a man. Confronting problems head-on is another. These are all things God the Father values in character—male or female.

I've heard it said that character is who you are when no one is looking. I think one's character is always evolving and, hopefully, growing, and we can help our boys shape their character.

Family Heritage

I saw a movie recently that initiated men into knight-hood by having them take an oath: "Walk upright and just. Protect those who cannot protect themselves." It reminded me of my own family heritage. I have a T-shirt that says, "Chisholm. A Scottish family surname. The name of a famous Western trail. A famous castle in Scotland. But more importantly, a part of my heritage." We study our family history to learn about where we come from. And sometimes we can be proud. Sometimes we can learn from it. But boys need a heritage—something to live up to.

My boys and I go out on "dates" periodically. We go partly to have fun and partly so I can teach them how to behave in public and how they should behave someday when they take girls out. I let them pay the check, hold the door, order, teach them to put their napkins in their laps. They are in training to be men someday, and training is a lot of fun!

Both boys knew that when they turn 13, we will have the normal parties, but we will also go out on a special date—just me and the birthday boy. The date includes dinner on the beach at a fancy restaurant, getting all dressed up, and a special gift—a Celtic ring with four symbols on it for Character, Chastity, Christlikeness, and Commitment. Each boy and I discuss the importance of each of the four Cs. All of these things are gifts he will be able to share with his future wife and children, and each quality is equally important to who he is becoming as a man modeling God the Father. It was our way of moving him into knighthood with him taking an oath that is important to his heritage—who he is and who he is becoming.

I know the Celtic ring will be a reminder of the night, that oath to character, chastity, Christlikeness, and commitment, and my sons will remember where they came from and where there are going.

Delayed Gratification

I remember when I was just out of college, I was traveling with some friends to Hilton Head Island in South Carolina. We ran across a fisherman who could have stepped right out of a painting of the Old South; bare feet dangling off the side of a bridge, fishing poles tossed in the water, and a handwritten sign on planks of old wood that read "Fresh Fish for Sale." One of my friends was a photographer, and she absolutely insisted we stop and get black and white photos of him. The pace of life was much slower than our Southern California lifestyle. I remember striking up a conversation with the local fisherman and bubbling on about my plans to go to graduate school and then work in a big corporation in Los Angeles. He took a long pause from his fishing project and simply and slowly said one thing. "Why?"

I didn't have an answer to that. I guess I just always knew that going to college is what I had always planned on. Now that I know all the statistics about what makes a successful young man and what can lead to his downfall and fulfilling all the doomsday prophecies for sons of single moms, I appreciate the importance of getting an education—either in college or trade school or apprenticeship. The military used to have a commercial that urged boys to "Be all you can be!" Looking back, that should have been my answer to his "why" question.

My boys both know that they can be truck drivers or doctors, lawyers or electricians, they can clean the sewers if that is what fulfills their passion in life and makes them all they can be. Whatever they decide to do, they must com-

Whatever they decide to do, they must complete college first. Then they can go to sewer cleaning trade school if they want.

plete college first. Then they can go to sewer cleaning trade school if they want. My concern is not so much the education as it is the learning experience of delayed gratification.

I hear them saying they want a dirt bike, they want a PlayStation, they want a new surfboard, they want . . . fill in the blank. It's all immediate—just like the video games and TV shows that consume our culture (and my boys) today. It's all instant. But life is not instant. Accomplishing things like getting your degree, buying a house, providing for a family, and being a good father all take time and do *not* pay off immediately. These are projects that drag on for years, and the boys need to know how to persevere through the highs and lows to get to the payoff at the end: the house, the degree, the great kids raised right to have their own great kids someday.

Maybe college isn't your training ground. But help them pick big goals they can expect to accomplish and start drilling it into them early. Since college is ours, when they want to buy that instant video game, we have the opportunity to talk about saving for college. And tithing. It helps bring up those opportunities to teach them about making long-term goals for their lives and thinking beyond the immediate.

These sorts of lessons will help them in every area of their lives as they face peer pressure regarding sex, for instance. If they have been raised to think and plan for their futures, you can help them realize that their actions in the throes of passion might impact their goals. My oldest son wants to be a Navy Seal. We have connected him to other Navy Seals so he can talk to them, and he exchanges letters with one serving in Iraq right now. He has toured the facility in San Diego, and we've looked into the requirements for him getting into the program someday. He's planning for his future.

When discussions about girls come up, and we have to talk about sex—a topic girls would find difficult talking to their fathers about and boys don't look forward to talking to their mothers about—we can talk about the consequences of sex outside of marriage in the context of his goals to be a Navy Seal and the impact having a baby too soon might have on his chances of completing training to be one of the elite fighting forces of our nation. Now *that* is something a boy can relate to and is willing to talk about!

Pursuing the Goal

Sometimes, in loving our sons, we must also persevere to reach our goals. My dear friend Chris is married (second marriage) with two beautiful kids. She also has a son from her first marriage. She was a single mom for many years and is now in a blended family. Her first husband was abusive and abandoned the family for a time and then came back into their lives after many years. While he was away and Chris and her young son were struggling, she met her second husband. He was a wonderful stepfather and role model. He loved this boy who was not his own, and until his biological father came back into their lives, they were close as a blended family.

Then the teenage years hit for her son and the biological father came back into the picture about the same time. Her son rebelled and went to live with his dad, hurting Chris deeply. He refused to talk to her on the phone, moved to another state with his biological dad, and refused to communicate with her. Although Chris was crushed and spent many nights crying, she never gave up on her son. She sent cards and letters every week telling him she loved him. She never missed a Christmas or birthday with cards and presents. She called him on the phone—even if it was only to be hung up on time and again. She pursued her son and never let him think he was not loved by his mother.

When Chris's father passed away, she made yet another call to her son to give him the news, expecting he would lash out at her for some reason, but still he needed to know. Instead, he did not lash out at her. He asked how she was doing. It was the first time in years she heard the softness in his voice that she remembered and longed for. They cried together over the loss of her father, his grandfather, and then her son

> **She pursued her son and never let him think he was not loved by his mother.**

asked if she would like a football picture. She says she restrained herself from jumping through the phone with excitement. Calmly, she said she would love one and thanked him.

Chris never gave up on her son. She very easily could have stopped trying. She could have blamed the biological father and lost communication with her son. That could have led to bitterness in both herself and her son. But Chris didn't make excuses or withdraw; she pursued and persevered. That is character.

This is the most Christlike behavior I know—to pursue your children with love. Christ pursues us. Chris is modeling Christ's love for her son. Even though he might not recognize it yet, it is being embedded in his heart. He will know and recognize real love when he sees it, even if he doesn't accept it. Chris is doing the toughest job in the world—loving unconditionally, even in the face of rejection, for the sake of the other person. Her son is being loved whether he likes it or not. And someday he will recognize it.

He doesn't stop loving us and waiting for us and showing us what real love is so that someday we might recognize it.

Christ does that for us. He pursues and loves us even when we reject Him. He doesn't stop loving us and waiting for us and showing us what real love is so that someday we might recognize it. The feeling of love will be familiar, and instead of gravitating to unhealthy relationships because that's what feels familiar, we will seek out the loving, healthy love Christ first showed us. When we find that love in people, it will just *feel* safe, right, familiar. That is not only true for you, Mom, but your sons as well.

Communication

Chris may have been at a disadvantage with a son rather than a daughter. A daughter might have been more vocal about her feelings in the situation. Typically, boys (and men) use fewer words and communicate less than women in general. When you are faced with these tough situations in raising boys, it's just that much more difficult to figure out how to maneuver when they do not communicate or respond the way you know you would.

Sometimes, as in Chris's situation, it is a whole lot of love and patience that wins out in the end. And sometimes it's figuring out how your boy communicates rather than trying to communicate with them the way you would, which is with words.

When I was in college, I lived on the property of the pastor and his wife and worked as a youth intern with high school kids. The pastor was an amazingly gifted public speaker who could move hearts and touch lives. But when working in a one-on-one situation, he couldn't string three words together. His wife loved him for it and gave him lots of grace in their own relationship. She had learned that he communicated his love in other ways.

I never really caught on to how a man so gifted at speaking in public could be so horrible at simple greetings one-on-one. It was great that it worked in their marriage, but he frustrated me, because I always felt as if he didn't care.

I collect Disney memorabilia and anything Walt. One day I came back to my room and there were little Mickey Mouse soaps in my bathroom. I thought someone was being extra thoughtful and had taken the time to notice my passion for Disney and even found soap. Another day I came home and on my bed was an antique Minnie Mouse. Oh my goodness! I couldn't accept this gift. It was too wonderful. I rushed over to the pastor's house and found his wife and asked her if she had seen who was leaving these gifts. I told her this one was too valuable, and I needed to give it back.

She hardly broke her stride as she smiled and said her husband had been leaving them for me. "He really appreciates the work you do with the kids, and these gifts are his way of telling you how special you are and you're doing a great job. That Minnie Mouse was his, and it *is* valuable. That's why he gave it to you, because he values you."

That day I gained a whole new respect for that man. Not because he gave me an expensive, thoughtful gift, but because he *was* communicating; I just wasn't listening in his language. Sometimes I catch myself doing that with my own boys. They speak a different man-language that I don't speak, and I need to take a minute and tune in.

My youngest has a special talent for picking up on things I show an interest in and getting related items for me as gifts. This tells me he loves me, and he is always alert to my needs and he wants to make me happy. Last Christmas I was looking all over for a wooden angel ornament for his teacher for Christmas. My son thought I was looking for an angel ornament because I wanted it. So he went out on his own to the mall and found one and surprised me for Christmas. It is my favorite ornament in the house. Another year I had noticed a pink cross necklace at a craft booth in town. Five months later, for Mother's Day, my son had tracked it down and it was wrapped and waiting for me.

Boys may not be the chatterboxes little girls are, but

they do speak their own special language. Be sure to learn the language and
cultivate it rather than trying to teach
them to speak only your own. Someday
this character trait of communicating
love the way my son does is going to
make his future wife very happy on
Christmas morning. I guarantee it.

> **Boys may not be the chatterboxes little girls are, but they do speak their own special language.**

Not Always About Me

When my birthday rolled around following my divorce, it was the last thing on my mind. My mom called
and woke me up singing Happy Birthday. I thanked her,
but I really wanted to just let it go. When I hung up the
phone, though, my little guy was crushed and started to
cry, "It's your birthday? Why didn't you tell me?" I hadn't
even thought that he needed to do something special for
me. I thought it was about what I needed, and I just wanted to ignore it.

The little guy disappeared into the other room in
tears. About ten minutes later he came back into my room
holding a tiny little box wrapped in a paper towel that he
had colored with his crayons. I unwrapped my present. It
was an old Garth Brookes cassette tape, and he had
wrapped it for my birthday. When I opened it, I exclaimed,

"Oh, son, this is my favorite artist! Thank you!" For the next year, any time Garth Brookes came on the radio or television, he said, "Mommy, that's your favorite singer!" Garth Brookes had never really been my favorite singer, but after that he sure was. Because every time I heard or saw him it reminded me of that tender moment when my little son wanted to do something for me on my birthday, and I had not been thoughtful enough to plan for that. It never happened again. Now, every Christmas, Mother's Day, or birthday, I make sure to have a plan so that my boys can shop or make something for me. It's far better for them to learn about the joy of giving than for me to be a martyr.

Filling the Gaps

One thing we moms are good at is overcoming adversity and filling the gaps. We become experts at taking an imperfect situation and making the best of it. Ours may not be what society calls "normal" two-parent homes for one reason or another, but we can overcome that. Luckily, we become quite good at it.

Coffee with a Friend

Things to Remember:

- You must go the extra mile, be more committed and consistent than the next person.

- The character traits you choose to model are what your sons will learn.

- Make every hurt a learning encounter to show them the character of God.

- Help your son set goals for the future.

- Pursue him, no matter what, like the Father pursues you.

7 Obedience & Behavior
Don't Jump Off the Roof—Or the Shed!

Rather he must be hospitable, one who loves what is good,
who is self-controlled, upright, holy and disciplined (Titus 1:8).

WE HAD A POOL IN THE BACKYARD at our last house. CJ was 10 years old and had a friend over to play. This was his creative friend who once led the boys on a treasure hunt to dig up my freshly planted herb garden! I was aware I needed to keep an eye on these two active boys.

Things got quiet in the backyard for a bit, and as all mothers know, that's a sign of trouble, so I went to check on them. The two boys had climbed to the roof of the house and were preparing to jump from the roof of the house over the porch awning into the pool. I yelled "Stop! Don't jump off the roof!" They obediently climbed down from the roof.

A few more minutes went by and they were quiet again, so I decided to check on them again. They had climbed up into the tree house and were preparing to jump a great distance off the roof of the tree house and try to clear the shallow end of the pool. I screamed, "Stop! Do not jump off the roof of the tree house! Did you not hear me the last time?" They replied, just as serious as could be, "You told us we shouldn't jump off the roof of the *house*."

With all the patience I could muster, I said, "Do not jump off the roof of the house, do not jump off the roof of the tree house, do not jump off the roof of the shed, do not jump off any low trees, do not jump into the pool out of or off of *anything* higher than your knees."

Little boys, you see, are very concrete thinkers. They need very specific directions. You may have already noticed this. Grown men gain wisdom over the years so they mostly know not to jump off roofs. Just remember that boys are not usually being malicious or disobedient; it just never occurred to CJ and his friend that they wouldn't be allowed to jump into the pool from a roof. I learned I had to be very specific and cover all the possibilities when I tell boys the rules.

Boys Are Active!

My younger son is a bit of a wild child. He is very tenderhearted, but to say he is active is an understatement. He is also an organizer. When we go on vacations or out for a hike, he picks up rocks everywhere we go. I mean *everywhere.* He collects all kinds of things.

A Biola professor I had for a class once had us students do an experiment. He had us collect rocks, and we carried them to class every week. At the end of the semester, he had us take a Sharpie and write on each rock a different sin we carry around with us—worry for my kids, stress about money, etc. Then he had us turn the rock over and write a character of God to remind us to concentrate on that instead of our worry. It illustrated the weight of the sins we carry around (for a whole semester!) and that we need to give them to God. His load is light. The professor encouraged us to start a rock garden, and I bought a stone

These rocks help Nathan remember the things God has done for him in a concrete way.

cross and integrated the concept into the boys' lives. Nathan collects rocks almost everywhere we go and puts them at the foot of the cross in our rock garden near the front door of the house. You can barely see the writing on some of them anymore, but we know.

In our rock garden we have rocks from the beach, the mountains, the desert, and from other states. We have rocks from just about everyplace Nathan has been. These rocks help Nathan remember the things God has done for him in a concrete way. We have so many now that they cover the base of the stone cross in our yard.

In the Bible, Joshua did the same thing to help the people remember what God did for them.

> And Joshua set up at Gilgal the twelve stones they had taken out of the Jordan. He said to the Israelites, "In the future when your descendants ask their fathers, 'What do these stones mean?' tell them, 'Israel crossed the Jordan on dry ground'" (Josh. 4:20-22).

If you have an active, creative boy, help him find tangible ways to harness that energy into a learning experience.

Concrete Solutions

Nathan also has issues with keeping track of his shoes. We've gotten all the way to the grocery store only to realize he had no shoes on. Once, I was headed out of town on a business trip when my cell phone rang. My parents were watching the boys, and they had gotten all the way to church and my son didn't have his shoes. Why they called me to help find them, I still don't know. But I've learned to create concrete solutions—like creating a "Shoe Box" which is a country wheelbarrow where all shoes go the minute you walk in the door. Then the shoes are there waiting when you're ready to walk out the door.

Morals are abstract thoughts, so it is my job to help the boys translate the abstract thoughts into concrete actions that they can understand and implement in their behavior. Finding ways to teach abstract morals in concrete ways is a constant challenge, and I have to be on the lookout for opportunities. It's not as if one day you're going to be able to sit them down and tell them and it will stick. As situations arise, I try to take the opportunity to point out the subtle lessons.

Ketchup Isn't the Problem

Often, as mothers raising boys, our guilt and remorse for their pain clouds our ability to teach them the lessons they need. My friend Becky says she feels like her sexual sin is the cause of her son not having a father, and she lives with the guilt of causing that hurt. When I mentioned this book to my friend Sarah, who was a single mom for many years and is now remarried, the first thing she said was, "The most important issue you can address for single moms is the guilt! Don't forget the guilt!"

> In our guilt, we often let the boys get away with things we wouldn't ordinarily allow, and in doing so, we are not doing them any favors.

In our guilt, we often let the boys get away with things we wouldn't ordinarily allow, and in doing so, we are not doing them any favors. I learned this when my sons and I were on vacation with a single mom friend and her two sons. My youngest was five years old, and my older son and one of hers were nine years old. They wanted to run on ahead down to the restaurant without us, and I was coming right behind. I told the older boys they could run on ahead but they would have to accept the responsibility of staying with the little one.

They agreed, and off they went. By the time I got down the hallway of the hotel and rounded the corner, my

Nathan was standing alone and the two older boys were nowhere to be found. I caught up with the boys and marched them back to our hotel room, and we took a time out. I had given them a responsibility, and they failed to fulfill it. My friend was back in the room still getting ready, and I told her what had happened so she could discipline her own son. But she didn't see it as the boys failing to be responsible, and she thought it was no big deal.

I realized at that moment that we had different ideas about what we wanted to teach our sons. I feel that letting my sons shirk responsibility in small things will lead to them shirking responsibility in bigger things. This was one of those teachable moments for the boys—a way to make a concept concrete for them.

Several years later, we were on vacation again with this family. I was cleaning up the kitchen where we were staying, and I came across a bottle of ketchup and asked the boys if they had opened it. If they had, it had been setting out too long and I would just throw it away. My friend's son said he did not open it, but I noticed that the seal was broken. So I asked him again if he was sure he hadn't opened the ketchup. Again, he said he did not.

Later, he told his mom what a big deal I made over ketchup, and my friend agreed. She made excuses for him and said it wasn't a big deal. She was right in the sense that the ketchup wasn't a big deal. To me, the big deal was that he was willing to lie about it. She missed a teachable moment because she felt so guilty for his pain of not having a dad in his life and made excuses for him.

Taking the time to teach good morals in seemingly trivial things will help our boys apply good moral standards when major things come along in their lives.

There *are* moral absolutes in this world. Just like gravity is real, there are moral laws that cannot be broken—whether or not you believe they are relevant. Once broken, the consequences can be grave. Sex outside of marriage can result in a crisis pregnancy and/or sexually transmitted disease. You might want to be your son's friend and tell him there are no rights and wrongs and he has to decide for himself, but that is not doing him any favors. If you don't tell him the consequences of wrong choices, that's just not fair.

I used to tell young women who were experiencing crisis pregnancies that they had the right to choose abortion, adoption, or parenting. That is the law. But it was my responsibility to make sure they knew as much as possible about the consequences of each of those choices. I told them that none of the choices would be an easy road, but some of the choices are less damaging to you and to your child. Those are the facts.

If you think you don't need to tell your sons it is wrong to lie or fail to follow through on what they say they will do, that doesn't change the fact that they will be seen by the world as people who can't be trusted or relied upon. It's just a fact. You are not doing them any favors by not teaching them and actively guiding them to mold their character so they become truthful men of their word.

> **You are not doing them any favors by not teaching them and actively guiding them to mold their character so they become truthful men of their word.**

The Author of Fatherhood says:

Above all, my brothers, do not swear—not by heaven or by earth or by anything else. Let your "Yes" be yes, and your "No," no, or you will be condemned (James 5:12).

Its for Your Own Good

Character always shows through over time. A person might seem very nice on the surface, but if that person is a gossip about other people, he or she will eventually gossip about you. People who lie in little ways about things that do not matter much will eventually lie about the big things that are very important. You've heard it said that the devil is in the details. The things you want to let slide because your boys have already been through so much will end up hurting them in the future.

Now flash forward to Blake and Brandon, the two boys of my friend Cathy and her husband, Ron, who is in jail. When Ron was home for that six months two years ago, Cathy got pregnant, and the boys now have a two-year-old little sister. Recently we were all staying at the same hotel because Cathy and I were attending a conference for work. Blake and Brandon came along and could sit in on the conference part of the time, and they took turns staying back at the hotel with their sister.

I have never seen two young men more attentive and responsible in handling a two-year-old, and they are still teenagers themselves. They were patient with her and never let her out of their sight. They played with her and entertained her until their mother got back from each session. Years of Cathy's parenting and her taking the time to teach them responsibility and character, right and wrong, obedience and discipline, had really paid off. These two boys were awesome big brothers, and I could see they were going to be wonderful fathers someday.

If you met Blake, at first you might not notice his character traits. The first thing you might notice is what others have described as an "edgy" look. His hair is dyed black and sort of spikes up in every direction. No piercing or tattoos, because mom won't allow that, but she is laid back about the stuff that is OK to be laid back about. You definitely need to pick your battles with your sons—and hair and clothes are not worth major battles. Hair and clothes are not what makes Blake a man of character who cheerfully looks after his little sister.

You can still be cool and be a parent who gives guidance.

I understand how tempting it is to let things slide and try to be a friend and the "cool" mom. Sometimes it's just plain easier, and we are tired at the end of the day and don't have the energy to make little day-to-day incidents into big object lessons. The thing is, if you take a small bite at a time, it doesn't have to be a big energy-consuming thing. You can still be cool and be a parent who gives guidance. What you value in your own life is what you will pass on to your sons in the little ways—like stopping him when he lies about opening ketchup. "It's not OK to lie. You can open the ketchup; that's no big deal. But you may not lie about it." How much time did it take to say those three sentences? You don't have to go into a big deal about how truthfulness is an important character trait and character is their most valuable contribution to the world and their futures, blah, blah, blah.

But just taking the two or three seconds to correct instead of letting it slide will compound over time to produce men of character. When you are tempted to "let it slide," remember what your parents used to tell you when they gave you a spanking, "This is for your own good! It hurts me more than it hurts you!"

Build Good Habits, Not Bad Ones

I've said before that persuasion requires repetition. Changing behavior requires making new habits. What the boys consistently see in you is what they will become. Getting into those good habits is just as easy as getting into bad habits; it's just a matter of practice and being able to recognize the difference.

> **One thing that single parents are warned about by every counselor and psychologist is not letting a child be the adult in the relationship.**

One thing that single parents are warned about by every counselor and psychologist is not letting a child be the adult in the relationship. Your son is a child. He is not the "man of the house" nor is he equipped to handle adult situations or make adult decisions. Yet it is easy for us, when there is not another adult in the home, to naturally defer to the son.

Some of it is birth order. My oldest son tends to want to take on more responsibility than the younger one. And birth order comes into play whether there is one parent or two parents in the home. But in your single-parent home you must diligently guard against expecting or allowing your children to take on adult responsibilities. You are the parent, and with bringing up a son comes a great deal of responsibility. You are the coach—the trainer—for this future man.

My friend doesn't consider anything a big deal. Her son is a nice enough kid; he just has no self-motivation because nothing is a big deal to him either. When you ask the mom why he doesn't get out, or why he isn't with the family on family outings, she says, "Because he doesn't want to. He's a teenager, and I can't make him do anything. His father (ex-husband, part-time dad) undermines me." That's just a not-so-good excuse for allowing him to think he's an adult. We cannot control what happens when the boys are at visitation with their fathers, that is true. But that is not our responsibility. Sons need order, and we must discipline our own lives so that they can count on certain things always being the same in your home. Athletes are disciplined. They work out at the same time every day in a routine you can set your watch by. That is discipline.

So look at it as our boys being in training for manhood. You and I had better be disciplined about the paces we put them through for their training. And "I can't make him" (fill in the blank with "turn the computer off," "not get a tattoo," "go to church with the family") is simply not true.

You have control over his training while he is with you, and as his parent you must create a schedule he can count on.

Has your son taken on the role of the adult making decisions of what he and the family will be doing? That is your role.

Has your son taken on the role of the adult making decisions of what he and the family will be doing? That is not his role. That is your role. Sometimes we just slip into the bad habits of letting them be adults, and we don't even realize it happened.

Just the other night I was on the phone late at night with a friend who had called because she is struggling with deciding whether or not to stay with her husband or divorce or separate. He has had several affairs in the past that she is trying to deal with, and the hurt can be overwhelming at times. He says he is a Christian, and she tells me they are praying together about their relationship. He also smokes marijuana and sees no problem with it. She sees a very big problem with it, and this is a point of contention in their relationship. She struggles with his being honest about it and they fight because she hates it, or he lies about it and does it anyway, and is out till all hours of the night—sometimes all night—drinking and doing drugs with his buddies.

While I'm listening to her verbalizing her options for keeping the family together, getting through to him, and determining what is best for their family, I hear her five-year-old say in the background, "When is Daddy going to be home? You need to get off the phone and call him. He might be drinking and driving. Call him right now and make sure he's all right."

My friend excused herself to respond to her son. Later, I pointed out to her that her son's behavior is a real red flag. It's not just the struggles in her marriage, or even the drugs or alcohol or the affairs, I find troubling. Why is this child of five taking on the role of an adult, handling adult decisions, even staying up late at night worrying about how an adult is going to get home safely? This is not OK. A boy is not a man.

The issues adults must deal with never shock me, and there is never one answer to a complex problem. My advice is always to ask the Lord first, of course, and then sort the rest out as you go. But when it comes to children taking on the role of adults before they are equipped and prepared to do so, you as a mother must change course immediately the moment you recognize the signs.

It can range from something as subtle as believing you can't tell a teenager what to do all the way to a five-year-old trying to arrange a ride home for his drunk dad. Just remember, your sons are not done with their training until they have become adults. Get it? If they are living in

If they are living in your house and you are the parent, be the parent and be the adult.

It is never too late to start. But if it is a radical change from what you have been doing all their lives, be sure to have a talk with them and explain what is changing and happening in your home. "Billy, I love you and I am so proud of who you are growing up to become. But I have been lazy in doing my own job of training you and giving you guidance, and I apologize. I've met a wonderful man and I've asked Him to become a part of my life. So you might see some changes in me. His name is God the Father. I know that may seem corny to you right now, but He is very real to me. And one thing He wants me to do is be the best mom I can be to you no matter what happens in our lives. I'm not going to be perfect, but I am going to try. And hopefully you will meet Him because I am showing you I am trying. There are three things I am changing right now and they are . . ." Pick three things that you want to change. It may be reading your Bible so you can learn more about who God is and what He wants for you and your son. It may be that you and your son are going to begin attending church and building a church family and you expect your son to go to church with you each week. At first he may reject the thought.

Children of all ages really want love and boundaries from their parents. Even adults need boundaries; children thrive with boundaries because they know boundaries mean we care about them. Explain to your son that you understand he wants to sleep in on Sunday, but it is your responsibility as his mother to get involved in his life and affect what kind of man he becomes, and this is one of the things you've decided you are going to do right now.

Do you think sitting in front of a computer and floundering with social skills is what he *wants*? You are going to have to be that motivation for him. That's what a trainer does! Tell him what he is going to be doing until it becomes habit enough and he absorbs the skills to do it on his own.

It's like riding a bike. No one *likes* to get out there and fall down. But if you don't actually get on the bike and practice, you'll never get the hang of it. Bike-riding becomes a habit. That's where the old saying "it's just like riding a bike" comes from. It's a habit that is so engrained in you, even if you haven't done it for years, you can hop on a bike and it all comes back to you. Guess what? My sons maybe weren't too thrilled to keep trying when they were starting out. But learning to ride a bike was a goal they wanted to achieve so they worked at it until it was accomplished. Similarly, being a man of character is a goal every boy wants to reach and a goal every mother has for her son. Show him how. Just yesterday I had to reprimand my boys because they jumped on their bikes and took off into the neighborhood without giving me a heads-up they were leaving. It wasn't a big thing, because they came home safely. But I didn't just let it go; it's not responsible behavior in our home to not let me know where they are and what they're doing.

By teaching the little lessons and practicing the merger of concrete with abstract thoughts, soon they will remember their shoes *and* to tell the truth. Be specific for them— "Don't jump off the roof, don't jump off the shed, don't lie over little things, don't lie over big things, don't shirk responsibilities you take on, your word is your bond." It will slowly and surely begin to sink in.

Coffee with a Friend

Things to Remember:

- Boys are concrete thinkers and need concrete moral lessons. Be specific.

- It is your job to instruct them and give them structure until their habits become behaviors.

- You are the trainer—the adult. It's your responsibility to model obedience and commitment for them so they can be happy for the rest of their lives. It's not your responsibility to be the cool mom.

8 Purity and Sex
They Need to Hear It from You

WHEN MY SON WAS IN THE FIFTH GRADE he went to camp with his class. When the class returned, one of the moms who chaperoned came up to me and said, "Your son was a well-mannered, perfect gentleman. He opened doors for the girls and pulled out their chairs. None of the other boys did any of that! The girls just love him!" And then she said, "I was so shocked because he is the only one from a *single-parent home*!"

I know she was trying to give me a compliment, but that label and the baggage that comes with it stung. Why would she be surprised that a gentleman came from the only single-parent home? Instead, I wondered why the parents in two-parent homes weren't setting good examples. But I didn't say anything; I just tried to think of the things I was doing to make a positive impact on my boys and how that led to their behaving *better* than kids with fathers in their homes. What impressed me even more was that my son had behaved this way when I was not around. That showed me it was part of his character—who he is—not just obeying me when I am hovering over him.

A Lost Art

I already knew my boys behave as gentlemen when I am around. From the time they could walk, I have trained them to open the door for me. Sometimes I had to help them with the weight of the door when they were little. And sometimes, when we approached a door, I had to stand in front of it for a second before they remembered. But over the years, with repetition, they have learned. I seldom have to wait for them these days.

Even when my boys were very young, they got up and gave their seats to elderly women on crowded trains. I've seen them stand in the rain to hold an umbrella while a woman dashed in the door to get out of the downpour. Many would call this chivalry. My boys know it is being a gentleman and that I expect no less of them. To be a man means to be of good character and treat women—all women—with respect. It starts at home with the way they treat me. And if they treat me with respect, they will treat others with respect. I hadn't meant for the fifth grade camp to be a test of my theory, but it worked out nicely that way!

My boys are living out their character so well that it could cause problems for other young men in their circle of friends. At work, one of the female interns recently left for college. She had spent a great deal of time with my boys over the summer. When she got to college, she called home to her mom to tell her, "There are no real men here at college, Mom! Not one of them opens the door for me like Dana's boys. I want a man like that!"

If I am to coach them into being great fathers modeled after the Author of Fatherhood, I must coach them to respect and honor women.

All women want a man like that—a man who will respect and cherish a woman. That is how God intended women to be treated by men. One reason marriage is so sacred is because God uses marriage as an illustration of how God loves His people, the Church.

Husbands, love your wives, just as Christ loved the church and gave himself up for her (Eph. 5:25).

That is quite a command. And those marching orders were given to my boys! If I am to coach them into being great fathers modeled after the Author of Fatherhood, I must coach them to respect and honor women.

Practice

As mentioned, an important aspect of coaching is to see to it that those you are coaching practice the concepts you teach them. The boys open doors for me so they'll be trained and in practice to naturally open doors for women as a matter of habit. I take the boys on dates to not only teach them how to behave in public and how to calculate a tip, but also to make these behaviors habits they practice naturally. Dates don't have to be at expensive, fancy restaurants. Some of the most romantic dates I've had in my life have been picnics in the park. Why not a picnic in the park with my boys for training?

When I was in college, I dated the most amazing guy. We never clicked as a couple, and he is now happily married with two kids. But I remember how awesome he was because he always opened doors for me and was always a perfect gentleman on our dates. I even had to ask him if he was really interested in me because after three months of dating he hadn't even tried to kiss me! Both he and his brother were hulks of guys—tall football players, great-looking, Christians, music leaders at the church—just all around awesome men. And they were raised by a single mom.

Their father had cheated on their mom with the secretary in the family-owned business and left his family to marry her. If you asked the boys who it was that influenced them to become the godly gentlemen they are, they would tell you it was their mother. In spite of the fact that as a role model their father royally messed up, both boys learned from their mother and the Author of Fatherhood what it means to be a godly man. They went on to have loving families and wives, and they will not repeat their father's mistakes.

That is certainly the fear most of us harbor, and what the statistics and society would have us believe about single moms raising sons—that our boys are doomed to repeat the pattern. That is just another lie of the evil one. Remember, with God in the picture, all things can be overcome. Our sons can see what marriage is supposed to be—as Christ loves the church—and then live that out in their own lives. And it begins with respect for women.

It Doesn't End There

"Oh, he's going to break some hearts!" I hear that all the time about one boy or the other. I usually respond that they already have. I remember myself as being somewhat conniving and manipulative when I was a girl—at least as far as boys were concerned. Now, as I watch girls make moves on my sons, I recognize their little tricks. I pulled some of them myself once upon a time.

Two girls showed up at our door claiming they were coming over to see our puppy. Funny thing, though, they spent very little time with the puppy. Then they asked the boys to go out and play football with them. Instead of playing flag football, the girls wanted to play tackle. Let me tell you two things about my oldest son. He's played center for years in tackle football, and he is not going to tackle these girls. And second, he knows that hitting a girl is wrong—and to him, football means hitting.

He has been trained to respect girls, and he would never tackle one. But they continued to push him into rolling around in the grass with them. One even "tripped" quite a bit and pulled him down so they could be rolling around in the grass. I resolved to go buy these girls a set of football flags.

It's not just a matter of training and coaching boys to respect women, they also must be prepared for the on-slaught of society and the women themselves! They must be prepared to explain to the girls in their lives *why* they insist on treating them special. Every girl is someone's future wife.

I talk with my sons about things such as appropriate behavior when they meet a girl's parents. What are they going to do when they are ready to propose—ask her fa-ther for her hand? Elope? We talk about all these things.

The Tough Questions

No kid wants to talk to a parent about sex; let's be hon-est. Kids especially do not want to discuss sex with a parent of the opposite sex. But if your sons don't learn the facts from you, they are going to stumble over sex on the walk to adulthood and quite possibly make some huge mistakes along the way. There are some excellent resources in book-stores on the subject. I purchased for my boys the children's versions of books on sex, and they have been reading those since they were five. There are age-appropriate, Christian books to help them learn about their changing bodies, the

> **For those who are stuck having to initiate an awkward talk, try to enlist help from a trusted male friend.**

differences between males and females, and what they can expect. Since they started early learning about the simple things such as "men and women are different because that is how God created them" and then moved to the reasons why and how they were different as they got older, the subject didn't seem so foreign to the boys.

But not everyone starts out on this at an early age. For those who are stuck having to initiate an awkward talk, try to enlist help from a trusted male friend. Or maybe supply the books for your boys even now and help them learn the basics at their own speed if for no other reason than they will have a reference to go to if they need it in the future. The only thing I do *not* recommend is just avoiding the subject all together. That could have tragic consequences.

Years of Experience

I have taught abstinence education in the schools for many years. On one particular day we were teaching to a continuation school. This is a school kids go to as a last resort; the students were some of the toughest kids I have ever seen. These were the kids my boys were statistically predicted to be. It was an all-school assembly, and as the presentation was coming to a close at the end of the day, one of the young men who looked to be the ringleader at the high school—tough looking, tattooed, and pierced head to toe—stood up to ask a question. I thought for sure he was going to say something inappropriate, call us names, or just make a big joke out of everything we had said. He was clearly hardened by life. Instead, he said something that shocked me.

"I just have one question." Here it comes, I thought. "Where were you when I was in junior high? I have two kids and no one ever came and told me when I started having sex that I shouldn't or didn't have to. Go to the junior high and teach my younger brothers so they don't make the same mistakes." And he sat back down. The room was silent.

Talk to your boys. Let me say it again on behalf of this young man. *Talk to your boys.*

They Will Listen

No matter what your situation, your boys will listen. Whether you are separated, divorced, have a father in the picture giving a good example or bad, or you are a military wife trying to teach your sons while dad is deployed, they *do* listen. I realized this with my own brother who was raised by our military-wife mom.

My brother and I have always been very close. I do all his shopping for him on the holidays, and he does all the heavy lifting for me. We've worked it that way since high school and all through college. I was ruthless to some of his girlfriends who I knew were not right for him. Then he brought Laura home, and the first time I met her, I told him on the sly that I knew she was the one.

When he was about to get married, I asked him to do a chore for me just as I always did. But this time his response was completely unexpected and stopped me dead in my tracks. I still remember where I was when he said it—walking out of our old house on the front porch, and he said, "Sure, I can do that. Just let me ask Laura."

What? He has to ask some woman if he can do a favor for me? Well, my mother had raised him right. He knew exactly who his new bride was in his life—first priority. Even my mother and I were second to Laura. And that is *exactly* the way it is supposed to be. The time will come when my boys make that shift in their lives too. And some new woman will be first priority to them. My goal is to have that woman—whoever she is out there—want to thank me for raising such awesome men. Start praying for your son's future wife now.

Romance your Kids

My friend Ann, with the nine kids, believes in romancing her kids. She has said time and again that she wants her kids to know real love from her and God first, and then they will recognize it from others. She demonstrated this recently by sending five of them on a hot air balloon ride.

Ann had planned a hot air balloon ride with her husband in 1992. The marriage fell apart, and she prayed to save her marriage for six years. But that wasn't what happened. The tickets she had purchased to share with her husband for the hot air balloon ride over the Pacific Ocean coast were close to their expiration date. So she chose four of her nine kids to go on the ride. One of the four came home saying, "I have been to heaven," because of the beauty of God's creation. The five who didn't get to go were disappointed and, still, in 2005 they were upset about it.

She decided to surprise those five. She told each of them to meet at her daughter's work but didn't hint at the reason. Ann then hid clues all over town leading them to the next clue—florist shops, candy shops, each with a disposable camera to take a picture of the five of them together on the treasure hunt. The last clue led them to the hot air balloon where hors d'oeuvres waited. At each stop they received a small gift to take with them—candy, flowers, etc. After the hot air balloon ride, they went home to find their mother had candles set up all over the yard and rose petals leading them to the backyard for dinner. Ann

Boys may appear to be too cool for outward signs of affection, but they always need you to make a big deal over them.

outdid herself romancing the kids. They never felt "not chosen" again. They knew without a doubt that their mother loved them.

Never think these sorts of things aren't important to your boys, because they are. Boys may appear to be too cool for outward signs of affection, and they may have gotten to the age where you can't greet them at school with a hug and a kiss anymore, but they always need you to make a big deal over them.

Shaving

I must honestly admit that I wasn't prepared for the reality of hormones in boys. I thought girls were the emotional ones and that the teenage years were an emotional rollercoaster for girls only. That's what I remember anyway. But both my boys started experiencing hormone shifts as early as ten years old. I thought that was way too early and expected it to become an issue when they became teenagers. But no, it starts young.

So get a book to prepare you to face puberty with teenage boys. It will be quite an education. There will be many things you have to become comfortable discussing, and one of the things you'll have to teach them is how to shave. I've only shaved my legs and underarms, but I was called into service to teach a boy how to shave his face.

Have you been to the men's razor section? There is a whole wall of shaving creams, electric razors, razor blades, disposable razors, beard trimmers, sideburn trimmers, and nose hair trimmers. It's quite overwhelming. I got a heads-up on how difficult this was going to be as I was watching a "makeover" of a man on a television show. In this show they discussed all the shaving products, and I was so glad they did! I wish I could find that on DVD somewhere. But instead, I decided to enlist a friend again—my brother.

One thing I had learned as my oldest boy became a teenager was that he wasn't as receptive to my direct attempts to help him as he was when he was a kid. This may be about the time when the seed to never stop and ask for directions takes root and begins to bloom in men. Any attempt to come right out and tell him something was swiftly rebuffed. I had to start sneaking help in on him.

I spoke to my brother ahead of time and told him I wanted to buy CJ an electric razor. When we were all on vacation together, I casually mentioned that while we were at the store maybe they could look in the razor section. CJ thought that was a great idea since he didn't have all of his regular supplies from home, and my brother was able to point out the razors he had used in the past and which ones he liked and which ones weren't quite as good.

I got CJ to pick one out, got a quick lesson from my brother, and we were off. All went well for a time. Then one day CJ tried to use his electric razor to trim his eyebrows between his eyes.

Now plucking eyebrows is something I know a little bit about, and I had been able to help him keep his unibrow under control. But one morning before school he tried to use his new razor to trim a hair or two, and I found him curled up in a little ball on the floor of his bathroom holding his face. I tried to get him to lower his hands so I could assess the damage, and that took several minutes of coaxing.

When I finally saw what he'd done, it wasn't nearly as bad as he thought. I tried to keep from laughing, because with all the drama he had created I expected an entire eyebrow would be missing. But when he finally let me see it, I realized it would not have been noticeable if he hadn't told me what had happened. But it was a huge problem for him, and by the time the ordeal was over, he had missed the bus. I just let him stay home to recover and try to fix his eyebrows to his satisfaction. It was absolutely what I would have thought only a girl would do—react with such emotion over an issue of appearance. But boys are just as susceptible to emotions taking control of them momentarily—even over a few hairs of an eyebrow.

As the dating rituals begin, and more and more girls start coming over to "see the new puppy," appearance is going to become more important to your boys. The way you handle yourself and the value you put on that is going to determine what they think is appropriate.

Adult Abstinence

I find it interesting when moms say they want their sons to wait until they are married to be sexually active, yet they bring boyfriends home for the night in front of their kids. If you have not made the decision to remain abstinent until marriage a priority in your own life, your sons are not going to see it as important in their own.

The Gatekeeper

I understand dating is not easy for single parents. It is especially difficult if your former spouse is deceased or not involved in the kids' lives, because you will have no time off. When people say single parents should not date through their kids, you would probably insist you would never do that. You probably wouldn't take your kids to the park hoping to attract people of the opposite sex like you might with a new puppy. Who would do that! But we need to recognize that because we don't get time off from the kids, we can easily fall into the *we're-just-friends-hanging-out* trap. You say to yourself, *The kids don't see us as dating. We're just friends.* But what happens when we aren't hanging out

If men always push women to go further than they want to go and the woman has to constantly refuse before marriage, why are men surprised when after marriage the woman is programmed to say no?

with that friend anymore? What the kids see is a string of friends who have abandoned them. And that is dating through your kids. For boys, this also sets an example of failed relationships as the way men behave. That is not the model the Author of Fatherhood gave us. He gave us a model of consistency. Every decision we make regarding our dating lives our kids will see as acceptable behavior.

Are you staying out all night? Is that what you expect from them?

I dated a man many years ago who never pushed sex. We discussed that we would wait until marriage to have sex and how far was too far, and that was the end of the discussion. I never had to tell him no and take on the role of gatekeeper due to his pushing me to go a little further each time we were alone. He was the gatekeeper in our physical relationship. I thought then that it was a very wise thing for him to do. My theory is that if men always push women to go further than they want to

go and the woman has to constantly refuse before marriage, why are men surprised when after marriage the
woman is programmed to say no? They are the ones who
programmed that response.

When my boys get married, and someday when I get
married again, sex is designed to be a great thing created
by God and enjoyed. My boys should not train their future
wives to tell them no all the time!

Coffee with a Friend

Things to Remember:

- Hormones and emotions are real for boys.

- Boys need to learn the facts early—from you.

- Don't date through your boys. They will model their dating behaviors after you.

- Boys should be the gatekeepers in their relationships.

- Habits form behaviors. Make sure your habits reflect self respect and respect for others.

- Teach your son to open the door for you and teach him how to behave on a date.

9 He Will Live It!

*Raise a Child in the Way He Should Go
and He Will Not Depart from It*

I RAN INTO A FRIEND AT CHURCH who is a single mom with one seven-year-old son. We started catching up on our boys, and she was telling me stories similar to the ones I've been sharing in this book. She expressed that it was her son's desire to have a father. I suggested she point out to him that he had a Father, and she jumped in, "I know there's God the Father and all that, but I mean what should I tell him when he wants a *real* father?"

The Author of Fatherhood is a Real Father

If you believe the Author of Fatherhood is real, your sons will believe He is real. There is no way around it. When your attitude is that He is real, rather than "Yeah, but we need a real one," they will have confidence that He is real and they will live it.

As my oldest turned ten years old, he began noticing girls and the girls began noticing him. I wasn't ready for it yet; he was still so young. The e-mail started, and I became worried. So we set boundaries again. One boundary was that I would check his e-mail. What I discovered was yet another reason to be proud of my son. The character traits I had been trying to teach him had made an impact. And now he was sharing and helping others.

A little girlfriend of his was struggling because her parents were going through a divorce. She had been confiding in my son about the regular stuff—her mom was dating all the time and she didn't know how to handle it. Her dad wasn't around, and she was hurt because he didn't love her anymore. The young girl was writing to CJ because her father was going to marry a woman he barely knew, and she hated it and she didn't want to go to the wedding, but she didn't want to hurt her father either. CJ wrote this, "I know he disappoints you. But I know a Father who never disappoints me. He never lets me down. You can talk to him; He won't let you down either."

> "I know he disappoints you. But I know a Father who never disappoints me. He never lets me down. You can talk to him; He won't let you down either."

My son got it! Now he was even helping others understand that God the Father is real.

Living Proof

We've talked about all the sons who have grown up to be fine men, husbands, and fathers—my brother, Ann's boys, Cathy's kids—and I think my own are pretty great. I've talked to work associates, men in high-ranking political positions, and pastors of churches who have grown up to be fine men in spite of not having a dad with skin on in their homes. I remember the first time I went out to dinner with Cathy's two sons, Blake and Brandon, after a conference we were attending. The two young men had insisted on taking their mother and me out to dinner. We found a wonderful steak house, and I was impressed that these young men had started their own business as entrepreneurs and had their own credit cards. When we arrived at the restaurant and Blake stepped up to open my door, I smiled and congratulated Cathy.

Great Fathers and Brothers

Another conference we attended together lasted several days, and Cathy had brought her little two-year-old daughter as well as her sons. While one boy attended the conference with his mom, the other babysat their two-year-old sister. As I watched these two grown men take care of this petite, precocious two-year-old, I could see they were going to be wonderful fathers someday. They were already wonderful brothers. They were kind and patient with her. She was spoiled by her brothers, I could tell. They were protective and responsible with her—living proof that moms can raise great sons.

Protecting Mom

Recently Ann, my friend with nine kids, was doing some work for me. She was late arriving, and we chatted about what had delayed her. "I had to meet my son for breakfast and set him straight on one or two things," she said. One of her boys had gone to his sister and told her not to take any more money from their mom for college. He was concerned that his mom wasn't rich and shouldn't be spending money on all the kids for college and other expenses. Ann got together with him to explain that it was not his place to say that to his sister.

I so admire Ann, because when she has to have those talks with her kids, she always makes a point to do it in person. Recently, she made a ten-hour drive to Arizona to talk to one of her kids over dinner and then turned right around and drove ten hours to get back here to work. That says to me that she raised them well and modeled commitment to them, and I pointed out to Ann that now her son was simply doing what she trained him to do—look out for his mother. She was right to remind him of the boundaries, but she could be proud of herself for raising a man that was willing to protect her. Her teaching had sunk in.

Coffee with a Friend

Things to Remember:

- They will pass on to their own kids what you teach them.

- Your sons will live according to the values you give them.

- You can be confident in the job you are doing.

- God is a real Father, and if you believe it and live it, your sons will believe it and live it.

- They will not depart from it.

10 Do You Know a Mom Raising Boys?

You Can Play an Important Role

Therefore my dear brothers, stand firm. Let nothing move you. Always give yourself fully to the work of the Lord, because you know that your labor in the Lord is not in vain (1 Cor. 15:58).

MAYBE YOU'RE READING THIS because your daughter is a single mom or there are women in your church you would like to reach out to. Maybe you used to be a single mom, and now you are married again, or a teacher with a mix of kids in your class. You are much needed in the lives of the boys these moms are raising.

Mother's Day

Just as Father's Day can bring unique hurts of its own, Mother's Day presents its own problems. Sometimes moms are overlooked because there is not someone in the home to help the kids celebrate. And sometimes, even though the kids want to remember Mom, all they have to give are handmade items, and at some point they realize their gifts are not the same as other moms get. This makes the kids feel left out and different, yet again.

Last year, my church held a very special event the day before Mother's Day and invited single moms and Navy wives, who are also often overlooked "single moms." We held a breakfast at a local restaurant for the mothers and gave them each a copy of Pam Ferral's *Devotionals for Busy Mom's* while an army of volunteers took their kids shopping for Mother's Day gifts at Wal-Mart across the street. The kids were all given gift cards purchased with money donated from the church and Wal*Mart. Then the kids were brought back to the parking lot of the restaurant where the moms were eating and a tent was set up with more volunteers who helped the kids wrap the presents and make cards. Another volunteer brought flowers for the kids to make a bouquet for each mom. When the moms were finished visiting and having breakfast as guests of the church, they went out to pick up their kids and were given their flowers and gifts—all surprises from the kids. The kids were beaming with excitement to give their moms *real* presents. This outreach event benefited everyone involved—including (or maybe especially) the church congregation. The next day the church featured a slide show of the event during the morning service. There wasn't a dry eye. Caring for orphans and widows was made real.

> **The kids were beaming with excitement to give their moms *real* presents.**

The idea for this event had been brewing in the back of my mind for a couple of years. I expressed it to my pastor, Chico, and he decided to run with it. Because it was somewhat spur-of-the-moment, the event had not been budgeted, so at first Chico was going to have all the moms come and bring money for the kids to spend and pay for their own meals. I pleaded with him to try and make the event free because I know that single moms do not have money for something like this, although the gesture of providing volunteers to help with shopping and surprising the moms was great.

I worried all night about how I could find a way to pay for this so the moms would not have to. In the meantime, Chico had already decided that the church would pay for everything. He just didn't know how yet. The next Sunday morning, he mentioned the project to the congregation in the first service and announced that we were moving forward with it and would figure out the finances later. When the first service ended, church members spontaneously started giving Chico checks to cover the single mom's expenses for

> I firmly believe that individuals in the church *want* to care for the orphans and widows, but they don't know how to go about it.

their special day. In the time it took for Chico to walk to the back of the sanctuary, he had been given more than $1,500 for the single moms' day.

I always attend the last service of the day because we are usually running late. So when Chico announced what had happened, I cried right there in the pew. And the people in the congregation gave more and more and more.

I firmly believe that individuals in the church *want* to care for the orphans and widows, but they don't know how to go about it. When given the chance, people want to reach out and help these unique families.

My favorite part of that special day was when I retreated to a corner of the restaurant and watched some of the married women in our church sit down with the single moms, talking and laughing with them. Some of those married ladies had been single moms themselves at one time. Across the street, their husbands were helping children shop for their moms. I have never seen anything more precious in my life than those burly men helping those tiny little hands wrap the perfect presents they had picked out.

Most of the presents had been ripped open as soon as the moms walked out to pick up their kids. They boys and girls were so excited to give their moms the gifts, they could hardly wait. That was the perfect present for me!

Be an Encourager

Many of the moms we invited that day were clients of the local crisis pregnancy center. If I could give one word of advice to any woman wishing to reach out to a single mom it would be "Don't pity her."

Often, when there is a death in someone's family, we don't know what to say to the grieving relatives. Pastors tell me the best thing to say is simply, "I'm sorry" and be available to listen if they need to talk. It's the same when speaking to a single mom raising boys on her own. Don't try to fix it for her or show her pity for her situation. If there is a real need expressed, meet it. But if she is handling her circumstances well, tell her so. Introduce her to the Author of Fatherhood and congratulate her on being a hero who is raising future fathers and husbands.

Be a Safe Haven

I have the unique opportunity to work out of my home, so I get to be here before and after school for my boys. My friend Ann has a friend who lives close to her boys' school. Be a safe haven for the boys in your neighborhood if a single mom has to work long hours and can't be home with her sons. Let your home be the place everyone wants to hang out. If you have a two-parent home, that is a great bonus because your husband can be an example for boys who don't have an involved dad.

> Just because you're a single mom yourself doesn't mean you can't lend a helping hand.

I once lived just two doors down from an elementary school. A single mom friend worked odd shifts in a nursing home and had to leave at 5 A.M. or even earlier some days. The daycare at the school didn't open till 6:30, so she dropped her son off at my house and I walked him to school later. Maybe you can be that resource for a mom who needs the help. Just because you're a single mom yourself doesn't mean you can't lend a helping hand.

Start a Small Group for Coffee with a Friend

There are study questions online to spark discussion and shared stories of your own. Find one mom raising boys (or two) and get together a couple of weeks and share. Don't make the commitment long-term for many weeks; we are all busy, and if you make it a few weeks at a time, it gives you a chance to renew, find the next thing to discuss and share together, and add people to your little group.

If you can meet while the kids are in school, that's great. But if not, remember that finding childcare and finding time are the two things that keep most single moms from getting into a small group. This much I have learned from talking to moms. Maybe you could meet in someone's home for coffee and have a book club to discuss this or other books. Figure a way to bring kids with you to play in the other room.

Or if you have a house, maybe you can offer your home and have babysitting in one room while a Bible study is going on in another room. Apartments are often small and make it difficult to coordinate watching kids and listening to each other effectively.

Share the Men in Your Life

If you are married, invite the sons of single moms into your home to experience your family and see you interacting with your husband. It's important for boys to see men interacting with women. When I was in graduate school, the time my boys spent with my brother-in-law and our friend Tolu were invaluable! Plus, it will give Mom a break.

My own family tells me I bring home strays. When the holidays roll around and I know of people who do not have a big family to spend the holidays with, I invite them and their children. My father is a warm old grandpa who does all the cooking on holidays and makes the best prime rib! Everyone is always welcome in his home—and guests always want to come back. My brother gets a little competitive with the family games, but I always beat him (not really) and we get to see his good nature about losing gracefully. Open your home and let them experience the awesome men in your life.

Now It's Up to You

If you were once a single mom, know a single mom, or are a single mom raising boys, it's up to you and me to reach out and give support. Society may not understand the unique trials, but you and I know.

We are the ones who have a heart for this, and we can use our own experiences to help others. Because this is heavy enough on your heart that you sought a book about raising great sons, I know we are the ones God will use to reach out to other single moms raising great sons! By doing that, we will touch the hearts of single moms and help them get through the day. We will be helping raise the great husbands and fathers of the future. Society encourages every form of self-awareness and support, and now it is time for us to encourage each other. God bless you as you raise great men and reach out to other single moms who are doing the same!

If you would like to get a study group of single moms raising boys together, you can download a free leader's guide for this book at www.beaconhillbooks.com.

Recommended Resources

Recommended Reading

Being a Good Dad When You Didn't Have One by Tim Wesemann
Boundaries with Kids by Dr. Henry Cloud and Dr. John Townsend
Bringing Up Boys: Practical Advice and Encouragement for Those Shaping the Next Generation of Men by James C. Dobson
A Chicken's Guide to Talking Turkey with Your Kids About Sex by Kathy Flores Bell and Dr. Kevin Leman
Devotions for Women on the Go by Steve Arterburn and Pam Farrel
Fathering like the Father by Kenneth and Jeffrey Gangel
The Five Love Languages of Children by Gary Chapman and Ross Campbell, M.D.
The Story of Me by Stan and Brenna Jones
A Knight in Shining Armor by Harvey Hornstein
Wild at Heart: Discovering the Secret of a Man's Soul by John Eldredge

Just for Fun (and for the boys too)

Left Behind by Tim F. LaHaye and Jerry B. Jenkins
This Present Darkness By Frank Peretti
David: A Man of Passion and Destiny by Charles Swindoll

Contact Me:

www.ForWomen.org or Dana@ForWomen.org